OPEN WIDE THE DOOR TO CHRIST

S. C. Biela

In the Arms of Mary FOUNDATION

COMMUNION OF LIFE WITH CHRIST THROUGH MARY

Second American Edition

Nihil Obstat: Mr. William Beckman
               Censor Librorum

Imprimatur: +Most Reverend Charles J. Chaput, O.F.M. Cap.
               Archbishop of Denver
               April 13, 2005

Published by
In the Arms of Mary Foundation
P.O. Box 271987
Fort Collins, CO 80527-1987
1-800-451-1321
E-mail address: inquiry@IntheArmsofMary.org
Website: www.IntheArmsofMary.org

Translated by
Reverend Jaroslaw Zaniewski

Edited by
Annette J. Higle   Michelle L. Curtis   Erin C. Rice
Anne Mary Hines   Joyce E. Pfaffinger

Cover, text design and artwork by
Ewa Krepsztul

"Decalogue for Faith Sharing" from Families of Nazareth Movement USA.
Used with permission.

**Dedicated to Mary, Mother of the Eucharist, our life, our sweetness and our hope.
We ask for her intercession for every soul who reads this book, that we may all open
wide the door of our hearts to her Son, Jesus Christ.**

Library of Congress Control Number: 2024950255
Second American Edition
ISBN: 978-1-93-331464-8

To our Holy Father Benedict XVI,
who reminds us that, when we
open wide the door of our hearts
to Christ, *we will find true life*.

Contents

"*Brothers and sisters, do not be afraid to welcome Christ and accept his power...Do not be afraid. Open wide the doors for Christ.*"

St. John Paul II

SPIRITUAL POVERTY AS THE WAY TO OPEN ONE'S HEART TO GOD WHO IS KNOCKING

> *"Behold, I stand at the door and knock. If anyone hears my voice and opens the door, [then] I will enter his house and dine with him, and he with me."*

REVELATION, CHAPTER 3, VERSE 20

E ven when we analyze our lives in a very superficial way, we discover that we are frequently so concerned with what we do and what we think that God, who is knocking on the doors of our hearts, does not exist for us. We are so immersed in the spirit of this world that it becomes an idol that makes us blind and deaf – blind to Divine light and deaf to God's knocking. The person who succumbs to his own thoughts and actions actually rejects the unique lordship of God. He ceases to remain poor in spirit. Instead, he becomes rich in himself. Because of this, Jesus gives a very fearsome judgment: "But woe to you who are rich, / for you have received your consolation" (Lk 6:24).

The one who is rich in himself also lives in communion with himself. Thus, no communion between himself and God exists. A twofold communion — a communion with one's self as well as simultaneous communion with God — is not possible. Rather, only the person who remains in truth about his human nothingness can receive God's Divine Everything. The poverty of a soul that is stripped of itself, the famous "*nada*" (nothing) of St. John of the Cross, calls upon the riches of God, or that which St. John refers to as "*todo*" (everything).

St. John of the Cross asserts that the soul has observed that life is short, ". . . the things of the world vain and deceitful [Eccl 1:2], that all comes to an end and fails like falling water [2 Sam. 14:14]."[1] You have to discover how false this seductive flickering light is — this longing to possess after which you incessantly chase. Only then will you desire to follow the real light that knocks on the door of your heart and compels you to become poor in spirit. This light frees you from illusions that coerce your heart to rule amid dust

---

[1] John of the Cross, *The Spiritual Canticle*, in *The Collected Works of Saint John of the Cross*, rev. ed. trans. Kieran Kavanaugh and Otilio Rodriguez (Washington DC: ICS Publications, 1991), 477-8.

and trash. It compels you to accept the unique lordship of God by following the light of His will. In this way, when you follow this light, you will discover the true pearl – God's Kingdom – for which it is worthwhile to give up everything.

St. John of the Cross stressed that after original sin the soul became enslaved to its mortal flesh, meaning that the soul is subjected to natural appetites and lusts.[2] If the goal of human existence is to be open to receiving what God wants to give to us, then being open presupposes the existence of emptiness as the inner space for God. This inner space is spiritual poverty, which creates peace in freedom from obstacles and disorderly self-love.

Because our thoughts should be directed toward God, all matters, even those that are good in and of themselves, that become the subject of concern and occupy our thoughts are obstacles that hinder our union with God. We cannot love without spiritual poverty. In this sense, St. John of the Cross emphasizes that ". . . for to love is to labor to divest and deprive oneself for God of all that is not God."[3] In this sense, spiritual poverty means to be stripped of false treasures that enslave our hearts and prevent us from following the call of God's love. Poverty is the only path that allows us to obtain the only true treasure for which it is worthwhile to live.

---

[2] Cf. John of the Cross, *Ascent of Mount Carmel*, in *Collected Works*, 1.15.1.
[3] John of the Cross, *Ascent of Mount Carmel*, in *Collected Works*, 2.5.7.

TO TURN ONE'S HEART TO THE ONE WHO IS KNOCKING

G od's "knocking" on the door of the human heart can be very dramatic. A person who is preoccupied with himself and his own illusory treasures, or that which contaminates the soul, prevents himself from hearing the sound of the Lord's knocking. Such an individual responds to God by saying: "Not now. I'm busy . . . maybe later. Right now I do not have time." With striking clarity this situation demonstrates, on the one hand, God's infinite humility as He patiently knocks on the door. On the other hand, this situation also depicts a person who arrogantly plays with the One who, despite the fact that He lowers Himself by becoming a beggar and knocking, does not cease being the Almighty God and Lord of all of the trash that this arrogant person accumulates, organizes, and adores within himself.

God's knocking is His call to you to turn your head and fix the gaze of your soul in His direction. He wants to give you His heart and, in this way, fill the emptiness of your human heart which is greedy for garbage. He wants to fill the emptiness that gives birth to sin, torment, and fear. Paraphrasing St. Augustine, one may say that restlessness torments the heart of a man until his heart turns toward the Lord and rests in Him.[4]

Original sin wounded our nature to such a degree that the attachments to which we constantly succumb imprison us. In truth, this prison is made up of our illusions; we are locked up in this prison because we are enslaved by our illusions. It is difficult to be freed from the prison of our illusions. Ordinary knocking is often not enough. In order to enter into this interior castle of our egoism, God has to forcefully attack it. He has to crush the barricades that surround the heart and reconstruct our interior selves such that our interior selves will be pleasing to Him, not to us. However, by resisting God's knocking and refusing to open the gates of our castle to Him, we make it impossible for God to love us as He desires. Thus, we choose our own meager and seeming happiness in which there is no place for the love that He desires to bestow upon us – the burning, passionate love that consumes His heart.

---

[4] Cf. Augustine, *Confessions*, trans. R.S. Pine-Coffin (NY: Penguin Books, 1969), bk. 1, no. 1, p. 21.

CHAPTER ONE

EVANGELICAL POVERTY AS FREEDOM FROM ATTACHMENTS

E vangelical poverty is not human poverty against which it is always necessary to fight. Rather, it means the freedom of a heart that has been delivered from illusions and can freely ascend to the loving God before all else.

The Lord says, "For where your treasure is, there also will your heart be" (Mt 6:21). To orient yourself in the direction where you can find the true treasure, you have to discover that all of the temporal things and matters in which we concentrate our desires are not treasures but only false glamour and garbage. Chasing after these false passions makes it very easy to become disoriented and lost. Someone who chases after the mirage of riches and is seized by greed and the desire to possess not only material goods, but also spiritual goods, becomes increasingly tormented. God knocks in order to show to such an individual that his only rescue is the attitude of spiritual poverty, which will give the tormented heart freedom from attachments.

"Blessed are the poor in spirit, / for theirs is the kingdom of heaven" (Mt 5:3). The New Testament acknowledges that people who are truly poor in spirit are privileged. Those who are poor in spirit use the things of this world as if not actually using these things at all; they remember that ". . . the world in its present form is passing away" (1 Cor 7:31).

WHAT IS THE PRICE FOR THE KINGDOM?

Jesus Christ shows us that we have to first become poor in spirit in order to obtain the Kingdom of Heaven. "The kingdom of heaven is like a treasure buried in a field, which a person finds and hides again, and out of joy goes and sells all that he has and buys that field. Again, the kingdom of heaven is like a merchant searching for fine pearls. When he finds a pearl of great price, he goes and sells all that he has and buys it" (Mt 13:44-46). Christ did not say about the evangelical merchant, who certainly had many things, that he sold only part of what he had. Instead, Christ said that *he left joyfully and sold everything that he had.* He got rid of everything. He became poor. If he wanted to hold onto something, then he would not have been able to purchase the pearl. The same situation applies to whoever wants to obtain the Kingdom of Heaven; only the one who is poor truly seeks the Kingdom of Heaven. His heart is free from earthly torments and desires; it is turned toward God.

In St. Luke's Gospel, Jesus states: "For whoever wishes to save his life will lose it, but whoever loses his life for my sake will save it" (9:24). Jesus speaks about losing one's life, thereby losing everything that is temporal. When we think about **losing everything to which our hearts are tied,** we may see that without God, we are unable to follow Him or to fulfill His will. The objects to which we are attached can be money, social status, environment, health, capabilities, gifts, or spiritual goods. Everything can become our material, intellectual, and spiritual capital in which we constantly try to find and build a sense of security, stability and self-worth. Through his constant knocking, God reminds us that we are not the owners of these goods and that everything we have we owe to Him. He desires to liberate us from this torment of possessiveness, from seeking support in everything that is insecure, temporary and unsettling. He points out to us the path of poverty, which is the only path on which we can find peace and freedom.

The process of *losing one's life* and becoming poor is normally long. It continues over a long period of time and, for many of us, our lives on the earth will not be long enough to achieve this. We can become poor in spirit on this earth by freely accepting the grace of spiritual purifications. Or, we can become poor in spirit after our death, in Purgatory. Either way, it is not until we redirect our gaze from the illusions of riches and treasures and turn our gaze to God that we will be able to find complete freedom of heart.

TO AGREE TO LOSE

God's constant knocking does not instantly show us the degree to which we need to be stripped or the ultimate price for the pearl of the Kingdom that we desire to obtain. God knows our weaknesses. Therefore, through various events He knocks and usually suggests that we give up only a small portion of what He has given us, such as some material goods.

Unfortunately, for many of us, giving up material goods seems to be too difficult. Such difficulty leads us to bargain with the Lord for many years, often until we die. This so happens because, even though it is difficult for us to call ourselves "rich," we still quickly become accustomed to a particular lifestyle such that we cannot imagine lowering our standard of living. Frequently we are enslaved by what appear to be only small and innocent attachments. In addition, however, we may be rich in desires, full of pretenses, and trapped by the greedy desire to possess things that we do not have but consider necessary for our happiness. Often, without realizing it, we become the slaves of our desires and we create, in our own lives, fears of the following: uneasiness, lack of peace, suffering, or even pain and illness. God's knocking, or His call to poverty, appears in the background of the living drama of someone who chases after the illusive mirage of riches and who lives as if God does not exist. We will not find peace or happiness until we attempt to detach our hearts from these illusive dreams and direct them toward the One who is knocking.

God's light tries to show us, who are so tortured by our own selves, the path to freedom and poverty. Following the path to poverty does not necessarily mean losing things. Rather, the path to poverty entails turning our hearts away from the things to which we are attached so that we are not enslaved by them. However, if our attachment is so strong that breaking free from all of the shackles proves to be impossible, then it is necessary to lose some of the things that enslave us so that our hearts can then be free for the Lord in the end.

In your daily routine, try to hear the Lord who is knocking. Through difficult situations that deprive you of the material goods to which you are attached, even if you do not know that you are so attached to these goods, God desires to give you the freedom of spiritual poverty. Perhaps you lost or misplaced something important. Perhaps someone stole something from you. Perhaps you were in a car accident or you lost a job that paid well. Try to see that this is God's knocking. This is His way of asking you to accept loss so that you may become poor and free for Him. On the other hand, God may also want you to take advantage of certain material goods. However, He still expects a certain detachment, distance and freedom of heart from all temporary treasures. After all, Jesus reminds us: "Do not store up for yourselves treasures on earth" (Mt 6:19). For the person who is poor in spirit, **things only have meaning insofar as they help him to fulfill God's will**. God, who is knocking, desires to show us how to turn our hearts from the things of this world toward the one and only true support – God's will.

Human nature clings to treasures and riches. It is full of greed and lust. Consequently, the attitude of poverty does not come easily to us. Losing is very painful for the *ego* and our pride. Each time we lose something, we have to overcome ourselves in order to accept the truth. When you go after God's light, which shows you the path to poverty, and you want to surrender something to Him, your feelings or mind may resent this action and suggest to you: "Do not do this because you will lose your life" or, "look, you are growing old, you are losing your strength, and you will not realize your dreams." Meanwhile, God desires that we continuously give up our attachments, until we give away our last penny in order to purchase the pearl of eternal life.

A person who is poor in spirit places his entire hope in God and not in the things of this world. Blessed are the poor in spirit because they acknowledge their own total dependence on God and they are open to His all-powerful love (cf. Mt 5:3).

We will better understand the kind of attitude that was described above, and which we are called to imitate, when we reflect on Christ's parable about the rich man and Lazarus:

> "There was a rich man who dressed in purple garments and fine linen and dined sumptuously each day. And lying at his door was a poor man named Lazarus, covered with sores, who would gladly have eaten his fill of the scraps that fell from the rich man's table. Dogs even used to come and lick his sores. When the poor man died, he was

carried away by angels to the bosom of Abraham. The rich man also died and was buried, and from the netherworld, where he was in torment, he raised his eyes and saw Abraham far off and Lazarus at his side. And he cried out, 'Father Abraham, have pity on me. Send Lazarus to dip the tip of his finger in water and cool my tongue, for I am suffering torment in these flames.' Abraham replied, 'My child, remember that you received what was good during your lifetime while Lazarus likewise received what was bad; but now he is comforted here, whereas you are tormented.'"
(Lk 16:19-25)

Up to the very end, Lazarus was stripped of material goods and had to beg for the things most necessary for his survival. Stricken with misery and hunger, he had to accept the sympathy shown to him by the dogs (considered unclean by the Israelites) that came and licked his sores. Lazarus finally ended up at the *bosom of Abraham*. This means that he did not rebel against his dramatic situation; instead, he accepted it and, in this manner, became poor in spirit.

Lacking something does not guarantee a person's salvation. Nevertheless, it does present a chance for salvation by making it easier to purchase the pearl of the Kingdom. However, it is easy to waste this chance when we rely on and place our hope in material things, rather than God. Normally, we fail to have Lazarus' attitude. Regardless of whether or not we are poor or rich, we resemble the rich man from the parable. According to the mentality of his time, the rich man thought that his riches were a sign of his particular chosenness. People respected him and, as a consequence, he felt exceptional in the eyes of God. He did not see the need to share with the poor, whom he considered worse than himself.

If the rich man from the parable had understood that he received everything that he had for free from God, then he would have shared generously with others. He was caught up in fulfilling his own desires. When a person is immersed in temporality and lives as if God does not exist, he becomes blind and deaf to God's grace. By adoring temporality, he does not see God's presence in his own life. Neither does he hear the Lord who knocks through certain events, especially when God's knocking is very soft.

The rich man from the parable felt that he was self-sufficient – that he needed neither God nor other people. Commenting on this parable, the Holy Father, John Paul II said that "The rich man was condemned because he did not pay attention to the other man – because he failed to take notice of Lazarus, the person who sat at his door and longed to eat the scraps from the table. Nowhere does Christ condemn the mere possession of earthly goods as such. Instead, he pronounces very harsh words against those who use their possessions in a selfish way, without paying attention to the needs of others."[5] The rich man, whose heart was full of the deception of riches and self-sufficiency, did not need

---

[5] National Catholic News Service, ed., *John Paul II, "Pilgrimage of Faith"* (NY: Seabury Press, 1979), 249. Pope John Paul II, homily given at Holy Mass in Yankee Stadium, New York City, Oct. 2, 1979.

God. He even regarded salvation like he did everything else – as something that he deserved. He considered himself great in the eyes of God. He probably had something in him of the attitude of the rich young man who was so attached to his material possessions that he was incapable of giving them away in response to Christ's invitation (see Mt 19:22). The rich young man *went away sad* while the rich man from the parable was closed to God's mercy, which had the power to heal and purify him from greed.

Is there not something of the attitude of the rich man from the parable in us? Do we not consider ourselves the **worthy** owners of the different graces that we receive from God? Do we not turn away from God because we think that we can manage without Him? Does God not continuously bestow countless graces upon us? God sustains our lives and gives us health and strength. Thanks to Him, we can see, hear and walk. God gives us the ability to think and to act. Are we grateful for these graces?

If God did not sustain us and bestow new graces upon us at every moment, then we would lose everything in an instant. Meanwhile, deafened to God's knocking and immersed in the spirit of this world by looking at the world without faith and constantly maintaining the absurd conviction that we gain everything we have on our own, we turn away from God. Do we remember that the work by which we make a living is a gift from God? Certainly our Heavenly Father is the one who bestows upon us the necessary strength and ability to make it possible for us to work.

Everything is alms from God's love. Do we thank Him more than just occasionally for these alms from His love? When we fail to thank God for these gifts that we receive from Him, we behave as if we were self-sufficient, as if our lives and the fate of the world depended on us. Is not a beggar, who is closed to his "knocking" Benefactor, a pitiful person because he has it in his head that he himself is a king? St. Paul asks, "What do you possess that you have not received? But if you have received it, why are you boasting as if you did not receive it?" (1 Cor 4:7). Why do we boast, even if in the depths of our own hearts, about our abilities, talents and achievements, instead of thanking God for these gifts?

GOD CAN ALWAYS EXPECT SOMETHING MORE

If your openness to God continues to increase, then He will gradually take everything from you. Perhaps His knocking will take the form of certain events thanks to which you lose your friends or the environment and surroundings to which you are accustomed. Perhaps you will lose your position in society, which provided you with a sense of security and self-worth. Or, perhaps you will not be able to fulfill your own plans concerning your education, starting a new family or professional career.

It is very important that you **agree to lose**. In addition, it is very important that you joyfully accept the concrete realities of the path to sanctity to which you have been invited to follow. Do not forget that the pearl you want to obtain is the kingdom of God's reign. Moreover, it is not a surprise that we have to do away with **our own wills** and give up **our own visions** of life in order to open ourselves to everything that is **God's will** and **His vision** of life. At a certain point on this path the "knocking" light can show you that seeking support in yourself is merely an illusion. As a way to purify you from this illusion, God may allow you to experience some type of physical or psychological disability, fatigue, or decreased resistance to stress.

The truth about your own weakness will help you to turn your heart away from self-love, which sooner or later can become a source of torment for you or anyone who concentrates on himself. When you think that you have renounced everything and that you are finally and truly poor, the Lord will look upon you with love and still expect something more. He may take away what remains of your free time or the possibility to rest. Maybe you will hear His knocking through some health problems, through changes in your intellectual capacity, or through changes in your ability to work. We must take care of our lives and respect them in a special way because this is God's will. If, however, for the sake of fulfilling His will, God desires that you burn out, then you will have to agree to lose your health and even your life for Him. His love wants to penetrate the tightly secured castle of your inner self; He does not want to stop halfway. Rather, He desires to be fully united with you.

A person who is poor in spirit cannot imagine any other rescue for him apart from God. Therefore, such a person knows that he has to call upon God with the greatest determination that he can muster up within himself. In the Gospel, the woman who suffered from a hemorrhage and was cured by touching the tassel of Jesus' cloak is the perfect example of this attitude (see Mk 5:25-34). Even though many people crowded around Jesus, she alone experienced the miracle.

Were there not many other sick people in the crowd who desired to be healed? Certainly there were other sick people, but they did not have enough faith and determination to experience a miracle. The healed woman spent all of her possessions and money on physicians and consequently lost all forms of support. Perhaps she was able to see in Jesus her only rescue precisely because of her lack of human supports. The woman was not cured because of the "magical gesture" of touching Jesus' cloak; rather, she was cured because of the deep faith that accompanied her gesture, which was a kind of inner cry to God for help.

In our own lives, the external ways in which we call upon our Lord in the attitude of someone who is poor in spirit can take different forms. Sometimes, it is sufficient to say: *Jesus, have pity on me, Jesus, I trust in you! Lord, rescue me!* Our interior act of will permeated with faith and hope is most important so that our call will not be left unanswered – so that God to whom we call out will come so that we may be united with Him.

THE LIGHT THAT DENUDES

Before you can truly begin to be open to union with God, certain defense mechanisms that guard the stronghold of your "*I*" against the Lord must be broken down, or at least weakened. The greatest obstacle to break down is the false, deceptive image that you have of yourself. Your fascination with this image causes you to **believe simply in yourself** rather than seek support in God. God wants to reveal to you how your idea of self-sufficient greatness is merely an illusion.

There is only one true greatness, one true love: God Himself. Only He can give you what you desire. By disclosing to you the truth about your limitations and by stripping you of faith in yourself, God seems to ask you to accept the proper image of Him that His light reveals to you. At the same time, He is asking you to question this artificially construed image of your own *ego*, which your pride is constantly suggesting to you. He does this so that by turning away from contemplating this illusion of yourself, you turn your heart toward Him. This denudation which God brings about in your life becomes a form of light for you. In addition, it also is a strong knock on the barred door of your illusory kingdom.

In order for the prodigal son to want to return to his father's home, he had to change the way he perceived himself. Only on the ruins of faith in his own *ego* did faith and hope in his father begin to grow within him. This is also true for you. God is frequently forced to deprive you of whatever cultivates and strengthens your faith in yourself. It is necessary to fall in love with the truth about our own weaknesses because, even though it is difficult for our *egos* to accept, weakness pushes us toward God, as if to send us to our knees. The truth about our own weakness and limitations that God's light shows us, creates a certain "spiritual pressure" that provokes us to cling to God. This spiritual pressure causes us to turn with an open heart to the One who wants to heal us.

Events that strip a person from having faith in himself can be God's response to a person's authentic faithfulness just as they can be His response to an individual's unfaithfulness to Him. In the lives of persons described in Holy Scripture we find examples of both of these circumstances. Out of love for God, John the Baptist wanted to lose everything (see Jn 3:30), and the Lord fulfilled his desire (see Mt 14:10). On the other hand, King Saul had to be stripped by God of everything and everybody in order to be rescued when he was unfaithful.

Because of God's will, Saul was anointed king by the prophet Samuel. Eventually, however, Saul turned his heart away from seeking God's will, and he stopped listening to God's commands. God allowed Saul to be victorious over the Amelekites. Saul, though, motivated by greed and human regard, was incapable of giving up the spoils of war. Then, the prophet Samuel revealed God's will to Saul, saying: "Because you have rejected the command of the LORD, / he, too, has rejected you as ruler" (1 Sam 15:23). How precise this statement is! God rejected Saul as the ruler, but God did not reject Saul as a person. Despite Saul's disobedience, God did not stop loving him. In order to rescue Saul from the pride of power, God wanted to strip him from his privileges as king and to invite him on the path to poverty. Therefore, the power of God's light touched Saul's vision of his own *ego* – a vision created by Saul's pride and a vision that compelled him to believe in his own greatness and might.

King Saul, however, refused to accept the light that strips. When faced with the possibility of losing his current position as king, Saul was willing to acknowledge his sins. However, because he did not want to give up the position as king, Saul begged Samuel to help him by accompanying him to beseech the Lord to turn away His wrath, "Now forgive my sin, and return with me, that I may worship the LORD" (1 Sam 15:25). God refused to listen or respond to his plea. Therefore, the prophet Samuel also refused: "I will not return with you, because you rejected the command of the LORD and the LORD rejects you as king of Israel" (1 Sam 15:26). Why, we might ask, did the Lord refuse to listen to Saul's plea? Perhaps he saw how strong Saul's faith in his own might was and how his pride of determination closed his heart to grace. In this case, the prophet's **resolve not to yield** was a **very special expression of God's love** for the king. Saul's salvation, and not Saul's earthly pedestal, was the most important thing to God.

John the Baptist was open to God's silent knocking, which called John to humbly lower himself. John voluntarily chose poverty and gave up the position that he enjoyed among the chosen people. In Saul's case, God had to strip him by knocking on his securely locked stronghold of faith in himself with the firm words of the prophet Samuel. Unfortunately, Saul did not want to accept God's knocking and, by clinging to his power, he rejected the chance for his conversion.

God did not give up. He continued to fight for Saul's soul. God knocked very violently on Saul's heart through increasingly dramatic experiences. He stripped Saul of his illusory images of himself. He deprived Saul of his friends, his faithful army and even his son. Saul had no one. When surrounded by the Philistines, Saul was left alone with only his armor-bearer. In His love, God had to take away all of Saul's supports, with the hope that Saul would finally reject the false image of his own "*I*" and humbly acknowledge the truth about his own helplessness. By treating Saul in such a way, God hoped that Saul would turn to Him as the only One who had the power to rescue him. Unfortunately, Saul's attitude – an attitude of great pride and faith in himself – prevailed. There was no humility in him, not even in the face of death. He remained deaf to the Lord's call. He refused to acknowledge the truth about his weakness. "The battle raged around Saul, and the archers hit him; he was pierced through the abdomen. Then Saul said to his armor-bearer, 'Draw your sword and run me through, lest these uncircumcised come and make sport of me.' But his armor-bearer, badly frightened, refused to do it. So Saul took his own sword and fell upon it" (1 Sam 31:3-4). Despite all of the previous situations through which God stripped Saul, Saul remained extremely prideful. He remained so prideful that he preferred to take his own life rather than consent to be humiliated by his enemies. In a **desperate attempt to defend his own miserable image**, he "took his own sword and fell upon it."

Even at the last moment, God did not abandon Saul. His knocking was certainly present in this great pain that the king inflicted upon himself. Through this suffering, God desired to open Saul to His mercy. Fear, trepidation, pain and despair might have led the king to finally feel absolutely helpless. Perhaps, in this last moment of consciousness, he opened himself before God, acknowledged his own weakness and called upon God to rescue him.

We do not know how Saul's interior history ended. We do not know what the state of his soul was at the last moment of his life. One thing is certain, however: God fought for Saul to the very end.

KING DAVID OPENS THE DOOR IN RESPONSE TO GOD'S KNOCKING

The examples of the first two kings of Israel, Saul and David, are very different. It was very difficult for Saul to bow down before the Lord, even though, like David, he was once no one important. Both of these men sinned against the Lord. Saul sinned by his greed for spoils of war and by his disobedience to the Lord. David sinned by committing adultery, murder, and deception by hiding the evidence of his sin.

The reactions of these two kings were very different when the Divine light exposed their sin. Saul is an example of the type of person who continuously and sternly resists God's grace. David, in contrast, committed greater sins, as is evident by his great fall. At the same time, however, David had profound and moving contrition. Misfortune befell them both, but in David's case, it led him to contrition, which was especially evident when he escaped from his rebellious son, Absalom.

David heard the Lord's knocking in circumstances that were difficult to accept: in the death of his son who was born of Bathsheba, in the dramatic conflicts between his remaining children, in Absalom's rebellion, and finally in the curses that Shimei invoked upon him. By accepting these consecutive misfortunes and humiliations, David opened himself to the Lord's voice that was calling him to conversion.

> As David was approaching Bahurim, a man named Shimei, the son of Gera of the same clan as Saul's family, was coming out of the place, cursing as he came. He threw stones at David and at all the king's officers, even though all the soldiers, including the royal guard, were on David's right and on his left. Shimei was saying as he cursed: "Away, away, you murderous and wicked man! The LORD has requited you for all the bloodshed in the family of Saul, in whose stead you became king, and the LORD has given over the kingdom to your son Absalom. And now you suffer ruin because you are a murderer." Abishai, son of Zeruiah, said to the

king: "Why should this dead dog curse my lord the king? Let me go over, please, and lop off his head." But the king replied: "What business is it of mine or yours, sons of Zeruiah, that he curses? Suppose the LORD has told him to curse David; who then will dare to say, 'Why are you doing this?'" Then the king said to Abishai and to all his servants: "If my own son, who came forth from my loins, is seeking my life, how much more might this Benjaminite do so! Let him alone and let him curse, for the LORD has told him to. Perhaps the LORD will look upon my affliction and make it up to me with benefits for the curses he is uttering this day." (2 Sam 16:5-12)

It is not difficult to imagine how degrading it was for the anointed one of God to have curses and stones publicly thrown at him, especially in the presence of his army and court officials. In addition, Shimei's accusations against David were false and did not pertain to David's true faults. David did not usurp the throne that was assigned to him by God Himself. David had the right, in the name of God, to punish this man for this injustice, which not only undermined David's authority as a king but also the authority of the prophet who anointed him. The accusations undermined even the dignity of God, Himself, by whose command this took place. Nobody would have been surprised if David had ordered Shimei to be killed at once.

Meanwhile, the king did not react to these accusations. Instead, David was able to see that God was knocking on the door of his heart through Shimei's words.

Upon seeing this so, David made an act of contrition and agreed to be humiliated by the idol of his own *ego*. Moreover, he agreed to be humiliated in front of others, as if to perform a public penance for his previous sins. By accepting this entire situation, this ruler risked being perceived by others as someone who is weak and unworthy of trust. Through such behavior David could have even risked losing the throne. In this way, the king turned his heart away from himself and sought God's mercy more than human regard. He explained the supernatural methods of his own behavior: ". . . let him curse, for the LORD has told him to." He stood helplessly before God, realizing his own guilt for his past unfaithfulness. Traversing the path of spiritual poverty, David contritely begged for the Lord's mercy and agreed to accept a situation that crushed him.

David stood before God with the proper attitude; He stood before God as a beggar. God enlightened him with the light of truth and knocked on the door of his soul through very shocking events. By assuming the attitude of the beggar who deserves nothing and to whom nothing belongs, David opened the door of his heart to God and stretched out his hands for the alms of God's mercy saying, "Perhaps the LORD will look upon my affliction and make it up to me with benefits." David would not have been able to invoke such an extraordinary level of contrition in himself and by himself. This was evoked in him by God who gave him the light that enabled him to see the truth and to have the necessary contrition of the heart.

Even David, a king, was able to accept the truth that God's Divine light revealed to him and stand before God as a beggar. Does this not prompt you to do the same? Can you not try to see that you, too, are poor in the sight of the Lord? After all, poverty opens you up to God. It frees you from becoming lost by creating a false kingdom of **illusory treasures**. Being a beggar before God, or someone who is poor in spirit, allows your heart to be free so that you may turn it toward God.

THE MOST PRECIOUS ALMS

Upon seeing his own spiritual misery, the evangelical beggar contritely and trustfully asks God for mercy and **accepts each form of alms**. Through his gratitude, he is open to God's knocking and Presence as it is manifested in different events, but especially events that are difficult to accept.

If the attitude of contrition were present in us, then we would be free from everything and we would gratefully receive not only God's refusals, but also the truth that God may deprive us of things that we have already received. After all, at any moment God can take away goods that we have been enjoying. These goods may include, but are not limited to: our health and physical strength, our work and livelihood, the gift of friendship, or even the possibility to benefit from the Holy Sacraments.

If you knew that everything that you have and are is an **entirely unmerited gift** from God, then why would you have to rebel or despair when God takes something away from you? Does not the One who loves you so much knock so that you might let Him into your heart and sit at the table with you? He always desires to bestow the best upon you.

When God allows difficult experiences to happen (for example: bitterness, failure, rejection, or disdain for being despised and rejected by others), the spiritual beggar hears Love knocking and believes that he receives **the most precious alms.** But, only through God's light of truth will you discover that God bestows upon you gifts that are the best for you. This is clearly evident in the life of St. John of the Cross, especially during the last period of his life before his death. At that time a campaign of false accusations was initiated against him. By the end of 1591, after a special chapter (series of meetings) in Madrid, the Vicar General at that time, Michael Doria, gave Diego the Evangelist a special right by allowing him to travel to Andalucia under the guise of a judge in order to gather evidence against St. John. Traveling from monastery to monastery, Diego the Evangelist attempted to acquire testimonies by force. He threatened individuals and made promises to them in order to provoke them to identify St. John's doctrine, even if momentarily, of being connected with the destructive theories of the *Alumbrados*, who were being pursued by the tribunal of the Inquisition.[6] This was done to cast a shadow of suspicion on

---

[6] Alumbrados is the name for ". . .a loosely organized group of spiritual persons in sixteenth-century Spain, condemned many times by the Inquisition, who taught that once a person attains the vision of God's essence in this life he can dispense with all external means of sanctification. Vocal prayer, the use of the sacraments, the practice of justice and charity, penance and bodily mortification become unnecessary. . . . Repressive measures by the Inquisition finally crushed the movement, which persisted in the diocese of Cádiz and Seville into the late seventeenth century." *Modern Catholic Dictionary*, s.v. "Alumbrados."

the Doctor of the Church and to bring condemnation upon him. Despite the methods that greatly bewildered and frightened even the most zealous of sisters, Diego the Evangelist was unsuccessful in finding the smallest piece of evidence that would cast even the least suspicion against St. John. Therefore, Diego the Evangelist went so far as to forge false evidence and falsify the witnesses' testimonies.

In such circumstances, St. John wrote to one of his friends (a friend who had assured St. John of his fidelity as well as expressed his own indignation against the behavior of St. John's persecutors): "My soul does not suffer in any way because of this, quite the contrary, it draws from it the precious lesson of the love of God and neighbor."[7] In another letter to the prioress of the discalced Carmelite sisters in Caravaca, he wrote: ". . . You already know, daughter, the trials they are now suffering. God permits it to try his elect. In silence and in hope shall our strength be [Is. 30:15]."[8] Looking simply in a human way at the faith of St. John of the Cross and numerous other saints, we can say that God treats His friends severely. In this way, however, God expresses His special love for them.

By living and allowing the attitude of spiritual poverty to take form within us, we achieve our ultimate goal, which is union with Christ as St. Paul declares: "yet I live, no longer I, but Christ lives in me" (Gal 2:20).

---

[7] Marie-Dominique Poinsenet, *Par un sentier a pic - Saint Jean de la Croix*, Ch. 15 (editor's translation).
[8] John of the Cross, *The Letters*, in *Collected Works*, Letter 30.

CHAPTER TWO

EVANGELICAL POVERTY AS FREEDOM FROM ILLUSIONS

O nly those who are poor in spirit seek the Kingdom of God. David would not have bowed down before God and contritely received Shimei's difficult insults if he did not have before him his sinfulness and the truth that his kingdom was like a burst bubble, which had disappeared and left him with nothing – except for God. In this way, the Lord God allowed David to stand in truth.

As long as the illusions, which God allows to exist, function, it is difficult for a person to believe that he is truly a miserable beggar who has nothing. It was a special grace for King David to lose his kingdom. In reality, though, he "lost" that which he never possessed. Therefore, David lost the illusion – the delusion that led him to stray into sin. Upon becoming a pauper, David was forced to stretch out his hands toward God and become God's beggar. But as God's beggar, David was no longer a pauper. Instead, he became rich in a special way. Because David was a beggar, God mercifully gave Himself over to David and sustained him. Because David sought the Kingdom of God, everything else was given to him (cf. Mt 6:33). Moreover, this "everything else," which relies on God's mercy, was no longer a delusion because David no longer perceived his own strength in it. Rather, he perceived everything as God's gift unceasingly sustained by His mercy.

After his rebellious son died and David resumed the throne, he was a different person. He experienced how illusory it is to rely on anything that is separated from God and His Kingdom. And so it also was for the one who sought beautiful pearls as described in the Gospel. He sold everything he had. What did he have? King David had only illusions, kingdoms made up of his own false dreams that do not last any more than do soap bubbles or castles made of snow. By turning away from these illusions, he received from God the kingdom of true value, the only "pearl" worth seeking.

The grace of God's knocking is a long and difficult process. During this process, God gradually, through exterior and interior experiences, convinces a person of the illusions he desires and after which he strives. In reality, you are a miserable beggar like King David, who lost his kingdom. If you accept this reality, you will become God's beggar – someone who is especially gifted. God surprises us with His proposal:

> *Give Me your illusions in exchange for the pearl of the Kingdom - the genuine Kingdom.*

TO BECOME A BEGGAR IN SPIRITUAL LIFE

The merchant of the Gospel immediately gave up **everything** that he had in order to become the owner of the precious pearl (see Mt 13:46). As a result, apart from the pearl of the Kingdom, he had nothing. He became God's beggar. As for ourselves, generally speaking, we do not make such radical decisions. So, God, who knocks very patiently, slowly, and gradually, strips us of our illusions and makes us poor. Ever so gently, He pulls us away from and strips us of various attachments so that we may become freer to choose only Him.

Being detached from material, intellectual, and psychological goods does not suffice in itself, however. Obtaining the evangelical pearl of great price requires more. God's constant knocking demands that you continually give up the illusion that you have any merits whatsoever before Him. It demands that you give up the two-sided illusion that, on the one hand, you believe that you do not amount to much before others, while on the other hand, you think that you are great in God's eyes because you think you can pray, you can trust Him, and you can be faithful to Him.

Agreeing to be stripped of the treasures that strengthen your illusion of being rich in a **spiritual sense** is incomparably more precious in the eyes of God than renouncing all material goods. As long as you feel rich in faith, hope and love, and as long as you continue to think that you are the lord of your own prayer and that you possess good will, you will not desire Christ to stand at your door.

You will not enter into the kingdom of your interior life and begin to act as He wants, rather than as you want.

When you discover and then acknowledge that you are incapable of having faith and trust, of praying, or of serving God on your own, then you will begin to turn your heart to the only Lord and Giver of all gifts. We have to remember, especially in this realm of our life, that nothing belongs to us. "Man is a beggar before God," says the Catechism.[9] Everything that we have and everything that we are comprise God's alms to us. We have nothing of our own. So, why do we still delude ourselves by thinking that we are rich? Why is it so difficult for us to accept our condition as beggars? Joseph Cardinal Ratzinger expresses a similar surprise, noticing that ". . . we do not render any grace to God, if we confess the true situation of our existence, consisting in our need for help, in the necessity of renouncing ourselves, in looking for a confidante and the possibility to beg."[10]

This same Cardinal Ratzinger reminds us that, when we say the words "*Kyrie, eleison*" (Lord, have mercy), during the Holy Mass, we relive what happened near Jericho when the blind beggar called upon God (see Mk 10:46-52). With this plea, ". . . we admit to who we truly are and who [God]

---

[9] *Catechism of the Catholic Church*, 2nd ed., (Vatican City; Libreria Editrice Vaticana; Washington, DC: c2000), no. 2559.
[10] Joseph Ratzinger, *Dogma und Verkündigung* (Munich: 1973), 123. Editor's translation of "*Wir sollten uns gar nicht zu gut dünken, unser Dasein so vor Gott hinzustellen, wie es ist, und seine Grundsituation ist nun einmal die Hilfsbedürftigkeit, die Notwendigkeit, sich auszusprechen, sich anzuvertrauen, betteln zu dürfen.*"

is for us . . . ."[11] He also points out that because we attest to the truth, ". . . we say: Look on me God, I am nothingness, but You are everything. I am poor and in need, but You are all immeasurably rich and able to heal all the needs of the world. I am sinful and evil, but You are full of lavish love."[12]

God loves the truth. Therefore, at a certain moment in our lives, God no longer allows our illusions of being spiritually rich to exist. He wants us to see and acknowledge that we stand before Him as beggars who have nothing of our own, and who are always in need of spiritual alms, such as the gifts of prayer, faith, hope and good will.

God's knocking gradually dispossesses us of our illusions that the time will come when we will be able to impress others with some achievements and that this will make us more significant or important in God's eyes. When you open the door of your soul to the Lord, you always stand before Him as a sinner who has nothing and who counts only on His alms. When God comes to you during the Holy Mass, in the Sacrament of Penance, during adoration of the Blessed Sacrament, the rosary, meditation, or any other form of prayer, agree to stand before Him as a beggar who has to ask for everything just like Lazarus at the gate of the heavenly castle. After all, is it not true that you cannot claim any rights to any form of spiritual riches? Before you came to church in

---

[11] Ibid. Editor's translation of ". . . es Anerkennung dessen, was wir sind, was er ist . . . ."
[12] Ibid. Editor's translation of "Sieh mich an, Gott, ich bin nichts, aber Du bist alles, ich bin voller Not, aber Du bist reich, alle Not der Welt zu heilen; ich bin suendig und boese, aber Du bist voll verschwenderischer Liebe."

order to kneel before God, you were away from Him for many hours. You forgot about Him. You were lost in your own thoughts and actions. You were immersed in the distant kingdom of temporal things.

By opening the door to God in response to His knocking, you recognize that you are the prodigal son who wasted his entire heritage. You have to admit that you are the pauper who suffers justly – that you deserve to suffer just like King David, whose unfaithfulness was publicly examined and whose spiritual misery became obvious to everyone.

Until you humble yourself at least to some degree, it will be difficult for you to accept all this truth. However, the alms of spiritual misery are extremely difficult for your pride to accept because your pride does not want to acknowledge that you are a spiritual beggar. Pride wants to continuously prove something to God. Pride wants to give Him a bill and receive payment, rather than alms, in return.

The evangelical beggar is not preoccupied with his spiritual misery or his lack of success in spiritual life because he knows that, on his own, he will never succeed in anything, let alone in this area of his life. The spiritual beggar does not worry that he will never be able to tell his confessor that he finally fulfilled all of the recommendations that his confessor gave to him, and that now he is Christ's perfect disciple. He does not count on himself; he counts only on the One who constantly wants to enter his miserable quarters and who promises to dine with him. The one who is poor in spirit

does not count on himself because he knows and accepts that he has to disappoint himself. Therefore, he counts only on the gifts that God's love brings to him.

When God shows you who you truly are – poor and miserable – you will begin to understand that the only thing that you can offer to Him in order to possess the "pearl" of eternal life is precisely your spiritual misery. When you allow God's light to expose other spheres of your spiritual life, you will be convinced that you have discovered a lot. You will see with ever-more clarity that you lack faith, hope and love. You will also see that you lack even good will and fail to entrust yourself to God.

Thanks to God's action, perhaps you will no longer be tormented by trying to find goodness in yourself. Perhaps you will begin to turn your gaze away from yourself and direct it toward God, who is the source of all spiritual gifts. God desires to free you from the torment of spiritual riches and to bestow upon you peace, which is the only outcome of spiritual poverty.

At the beginning of the path to sanctity, when the light of God's truth is not very intense, a person usually perceives a lot of goodness in himself. Many people consider themselves to be very *fruitful evangelical soil*, which is capable of yielding, if not a hundredfold, then at least a thirtyfold. Only after a certain period of time will such individuals begin to see that they are "soil" of not such good quality. Perhaps, they are "soil" that is fertile but contains plenty of weeds. After a while, according to the degree to which they progress in their interior life, they will discover with great surprise that they are *rocky soil*, covered only with a thin layer of fertile soil called humility. Finally, such individuals will discover that they are a *massive solid rock*, meaning soil that never yields fruit unless an authentic miracle of God's mercy takes place (cf. Lk 8:5-15).

The path to holiness means the acceptance of the true state of being a spiritual beggar. Whoever acknowledges that he is a *massive rock* on which God's grain will never yield fruit, stands before God with empty hands, begs for mercy, and discovers in God the only chance for salvation. Only when we turn away from our illusions of perfection and open ourselves up to Mercy, which knocks on the doors of our hearts, will we discover the chance to be united with God.

TO ACCEPT ONE'S OWN FALLS

God is forming in you the attitude of someone who is poor in spirit. He desires to protect you from the torment that arises when you chase after the mirage of your own perfection. The person who is poor in spirit is not tormented by the sight of his own misery or by his own failures. Even more importantly, his misery and failures do not surprise him. It is much easier for a person who is poor in spirit to acknowledge that his path to God may consist of constantly having to get up after falling. After all, does the Sacred Scripture not say that even the righteous man will fall seven

times and seven times get up (cf. Prov 24:16)? What, then, is
the situation of the sinner? So, do not be sad that you fall
again and again. Instead, focus on getting up right away. It is
important that you pick yourself up after each fall because
you are a child of God. You do not even have to stray very far
away from God like the prodigal son did in order to return
to Him. God is right next to you, knocking on your door.

Your right to be an adopted child of God was
purchased for you with Christ's blood. Therefore, do not be
discouraged, even when you experience your own spiritual
misery more and more. As long as you rise after each fall
when you are struggling with your sins, and as long as you
acknowledge your own evil and trustfully open yourself to
God's mercy, you will not lose your inheritance. The worst
reaction would be to give up and close yourself off from God.

You have to fight with your weaknesses. God calls you
not only to fight the weakness of succumbing to certain
habits that lead you to commit mortal sin, but also to resist
venial sins and imperfections. During a more advanced stage
of interior life, when you avoid any conscious and willful act
to sin, you must humbly accept the truth that God's light
exposes to you – the truth pertaining to that which is
contained within the whitewashed tomb of your soul.

God wants you to try to believe that, even though He
rejects all evil, He will never reject you as a person. Instead,
He always presses you to Himself because He is love. In St.
Paul's writings and in his teaching, he very clearly connects

the sense of his own misery with his dignity as a child of God. In his letter to the Romans, St. Paul employs extraordinarily strong words to disclose the truth about who a person is on his own: ". . . I am carnal, sold into slavery to sin. . . . For I do not do the good I want, but I do the evil I do not want" (7:14, 19). But, right after that, he proclaims: "Thanks be to God through Jesus Christ our Lord" (7:25). Our dignity as children of God was restored to us through Jesus Christ, who redeemed our infinite spiritual misery. It is precisely because of God's gift of Redemption that we are His adopted sons and daughters. Our complete openness to the gift of Redemption is the condition on which the privileges of being His children are bestowed upon us. This openness, however, is impossible without being aware of **how desperately we need the gift of Redemption.**

The helplessness that we experience when we are confronted with various symptoms of our own spiritual misery attests to how we are "sold into slavery to sin." This helplessness causes us to stand before God just like beggars who must constantly call out for His mercy because they see it is their only chance to be rescued. Such an attitude takes nothing away from our status as children of God. On the contrary, only when we stand before the Lord with this attitude of spiritual poverty can we fully discover our dignity. When we remain before God in truth and trustfully place all of our hope in Him, then **He can fill us with Himself.**

Our dignity expresses itself in the attitude of spiritual poverty. It is how **God's temples**, which we each are, **can be**

illuminated by the fullness of splendor. When you begin to discover the mystery of the whitewashed tomb more clearly, never give up the fight and the need to rise from your falls because these are the ways in which you can constantly return to the privilege and right to be a child of God. Your Heavenly Father counts on the fact that, even if, until the end of your life, you do not see any of the fruits of your attempts to struggle with sin and weakness, you will not become discouraged.

St. Thérèse of the Child Jesus spoke about this with her sister Celine in the following way: "If God wills you also to have this experience, then offer up the sacrifice to Him: in other words, if He wills that throughout your entire life you should feel a repugnance to suffering and humiliation, if He permits all the flowers of your holy desires and good will to fall to the ground without any fruit, do not worry. At the moment of death, your soul will be laden with rich fruits which, at His Word, shall have fully ripened in the twinkling of an eye."[13] Do you not think that you, too, should take the advice of St. Thérèse and offer to the Lord the effects of your interior struggles? After all, are you not "fighting" because of the One who is wounded by your sins, rather than because you hope to boast about the fruits of your victory? You should desire that God hide the fruits of your victories from you and, in so doing, purify you from your pride. Perhaps you ask yourself: "Would it not be easier to live this way rather

---

[13] Sister Geneviève of the Holy Face, A *Memoir of My Sister St. Thérèse*, trans. The Carmelite Sisters of New York (New York, NY: P.J. Kenedy & Sons, 1959), 37-8.

than to sin?" Certainly, the answer is "yes." At the same time, however, would living without sin not inflate our pride? For, our pride is continuously fed with a sense of perfection. This "perfection" causes us to hold ourselves in high esteem and consequently eliminates any possibility for spiritual poverty.

On your path to God, do not be surprised that you discover your own misery and nothingness more clearly. You should receive these revelations with joy. For, if you were perfect, then you would not need God. Only the person who experiences his own misery can turn his heart away from himself toward the Lord, who is knocking. This person calls out to God to come to him. When, with His light, God discloses to you the depth of your misery and weakness, it will become clear to you that you must ask Him to come to you first and open you Himself. Then you will understand that the way He knocks on your heart is not any ordinary way. Rather, the way that God knocks comes in the form of a "gift of light" by which you can discover the truth about yourself. In turn, this truth compels you to call out to God and ask Him to come to you and to open the door of your heart Himself.

THE ABYSS OF MISERY THAT CALLS UPON THE ABYSS OF MERCY

When we see the truth about our misery more clearly, we understand that we will never become God's beggars by means of our own efforts. Therefore, we must call out to God and ask that His action become stronger in us so that the power of His grace can penetrate our lives, strip us of all forms of riches, and make us poorer. In response to this kind of call, the Lord will bestow upon us grace that is more precious than anything for which we normally ask. He comes to you when you are lonely, abandoned, misunderstood by your dear ones, weak and helpless. He desires that you interpret these difficult times in the light of faith – that you interpret these experiences as a form of His knocking and as a call to you to have greater evangelical radicalism and determination to follow Him to the end. Thanks to these graces, you will discover more and more clearly the truth that brings you peace in knowing that it is not worthwhile to seek support in yourself or in other people. Our only sure hope is God, who is always ready to enter our lives with the power of His love. And, a crumb of consent is enough for God.

The evangelical beggar sees more clearly how miserable the shabby garbs that cover his soul really are. He perceives how they are filthy and reek with the stench of sin. He sees what his sins and unfaithfulness have done to the white garment that covers his soul – white like the one he received at Holy Baptism. Then, such a person acknowledges that he constantly offends God by his own life. In spite of this and because of this, the evangelical beggar does not stop begging for the alms of God's mercy. He does not stop begging, which means that he does not stop trusting. He believes that, while here on earth, the One who joyfully sat at the table with tax collectors and prostitutes will enter his house and dine with him (cf. Rev 3:20).

When acknowledging the abyss of our spiritual misery, we have to call upon another abyss: God's mercy. This is the path that leads to eternal contact with God, face to face. It is the path that leads to participation in God's interior life. It is the path at the end of which our human nature will be divinized. The Kingdom of God, after all, belongs to the poor in spirit – the beggars who trustfully call upon God's mercy. They know that they live only because of God's mercy and because they freely receive the "pearl" of God's Kingdom as alms.

When you understand that you live only because of God's mercy, then you will stop placing demands on God. You will quit presenting your pretenses and expectations to Him. You will agree to accept everything and be grateful to God for everything. Your heart will be filled with the peace and harmony that only a beggar of God can experience.

THE GRATEFUL BEGGAR

A person who is poor in spirit is like a beggar because he knows that he is completely dependent upon alms and that he cannot survive without them. As a result, he is not resentful under any conditions and is grateful for whatever is given to him. We should have a similar attitude in our relationship with God.

Why is it so difficult for us to admit that on our own we have nothing and that on our own we are only beggars before the Lord? If someone asserts that he is not a beggar and simultaneously claims that, because of the graces of Holy Baptism, he is heir to heavenly inheritance, then he must look at what he has done to the white garment he received at Baptism. During our Baptism, we receive a real treasure. However, we squander it. Therefore, we should feel like the prodigal son who was the heir to a great inheritance, but who returned to his father as a beggar and humbly requested, "... treat me as you would treat one of your hired workers" (Lk 15:19). Imagine a prodigal son who, having returned home, places conditions on his father: he demands to be served a feast and asks for the finest clothing, new sandals, and a ring. If such a prodigal son had really thought that he still deserved something after what he did, then would he have been received so warmly? If this had been the attitude of the prodigal son, then the father would have had to treat him severely, which the son rightly deserved, in order to contain his son's pride.

How do we behave before the Father who continuously bestows graces upon us, even though we are constantly unfaithful to Him? Quite often we place conditions on the Father. We are quick to see things that we do not like and we are frequently dissatisfied. Can we imagine that, after returning home, the prodigal son would have ever held it against his father if his father waited too long to come out to meet him? Or can we imagine the prodigal son complaining that the robe that he received was too short or that the banquet was not splendid enough? Even if we do not complain outright, our lack of gratitude is in itself a specific way of placing pretentious claims and demands on our Father. An ungrateful person resembles a beggar who is convinced that everyone is obliged to give generously to him, support him, and show him special respect. Such a beggar does not open the door to God, who is knocking. Such a beggar does not accept God's alms and acts as if he were to say, "Come back later and bring me something else."

In His love for us, God is as if blind to our behavior. He continuously waits for the time when we will receive His "knocking" light, which penetrates our souls, and for the time when we will stand before Him in truth, as beggars. If we do not do so here on earth, then we will still have to admit to our true condition of being beggars in purgatory.

Spiritual gifts are among those things that we consider due to us. Can you say that your prayer resembles the prayer of a spiritual beggar? When you kneel before the Lord, do you ask Him for the **alms of prayer**? Do you pray for a gift that you do not deserve at all? Do you assume this attitude when you receive the Holy Eucharist, confess your sins, or adore the Blessed Sacrament? Do you thank God for these graces? How often do we think that the gift of the Holy Eucharist and the grace of Reconciliation are due to us? Whenever we think that we deserve these gifts, or whenever we think that they are due to us, this clearly shows our lack of gratitude. Gratitude is the best testimony to the fact that we see the abyss of our own nothingness. If we fail to see that we are nobody on our own, then it is not surprising that we fail to notice or to thank God for His gifts. Instead of gratitude, we have the prideful self-certainty and the subconscious conviction that everything belongs to us.

The degree to which we are ungrateful is the degree to which our pride and pompous conceit offend God. Sprawled on the thrones of our own false kingdoms, we fail to see the need to open the borders of this "kingdom" to the only true, genuine King who knocks on the doors of our hearts like a beggar.

TO AGREE TO BE BRUSHED OFF OR EVEN
PUSHED ASIDE

St. Thérèse of the Child Jesus teaches us "to recognize our nothingness, to [await] everything from God as a little child [awaits] everything from its father."[14] An expression of this awaiting can be the gesture in which you trustfully stretch out your hands like a beggar toward God.

The evangelical beggar trusts because he knows that he is a beloved child of the most caring Father and King. He sees his spiritual misery very clearly and knows that when he stands before God, he is *dust and ashes*. As a result of this, he agrees even to be pushed aside and brushed off. Even though he stretches out his hands, he accepts the fact that he may be refused. How many beggars go without anything? How many people refuse to respond to their call? If we had the attitude

---

[14] Thérèse of Lisieux, *Her Last Conversations*, Aug. 6, no. 8, trans. John Clarke, O.C.D. (Washington, DC: ICS Publications, 1977), 138.

of a beggar, then we would accept any perceived lack of God's response to our prayers.

There are times when it seems that God does not respond to us when we plead to be freed from our enslavement to certain sins. Why? Perhaps standing in truth and discovering our own weaknesses is more important than our external immaculateness? Perhaps in this way, God is curing us from our delusion of thinking positively about ourselves, and this process makes us progressively poorer. God desires to teach us true trust and entrustment wherein we do not count on our own merits. A person who is poor in spirit does not have any merits of his own before the Lord. Our desire to earn God's love by the power of our own deeds contradicts the attitude of someone who is poor in spirit and also contradicts the beatitudes of Jesus Christ. The desire to earn God's love is a symptom of spiritual misery.

God cannot shield you from your faults or free you from your weaknesses if authentic humility is not in you. When you attribute the graces of being shielded from sins and unfaithfulness to yourself, it strengthens your false conviction that you are finally perfect. Your pride inflates enormously and completely closes you off from the One who is knocking. However, through the discovery of your weaknesses and unfaithfulness, you have a greater chance to acknowledge that you are only a miserable beggar who deserves to be left and abandoned by God.[15] Such was the attitude of the Good Thief

---

[15] Cf. John of the Cross, *The Dark Night*, in *Collected Works*, 2.7.7.

as he was dying on the cross. His attitude can be an example to us. The Thief's plea for mercy, "Jesus, remember me when you come into your kingdom" (Lk 23:42), is the call of a beggar who is tormented not only by physical pain but also by the realization that he suffers justly because of his own evil. When a person who is poor in spirit stands before God, he is like the Good Thief who consented to allow his evil and spiritual misery to be talked about by those surrounding him. The Good Thief did not protest when people made fun of him and derided him as he was dying on the cross. Not only did he accept this, he also acknowledged that he deserved everything that happened to him.

The Canaanite woman is another example of someone who accepted God's seeming refusal. Initially, Jesus did not respond to her plea. Then, He refused outright to fulfill her plea. Finally, He responded with words that could deeply wound anyone: "It is not right to take the food of the children and throw it to the dogs" (Mt 15:26). To compare someone who asks for help to a dog is a sufficient humiliation, even if one does not know that the Israelites considered dogs to be very impure animals. The Canaanite woman took no offense to this. Like a beggar to whom decaying leftovers instead of fresh food are thrown, the Canaanite woman accepted the humiliation in a natural way; she knew that she deserved nothing and that nothing should be given to her. Yet, she persistently kept asking.

The Canaanite woman's persistent plea to Jesus to rescue her daughter was filled with faith. Upon seeing her

49

dramatic situation, Jesus did not leave the woman's request unanswered. When Jesus appeared to reject the Canaanite woman and her child, she did not become discouraged. Rather, this humiliation only made her more determined and provoked her to beg even more. In a way, the Canaanite woman began to really beg. She became more persistent, like a storm, and, in this way, exposed the beautiful richness of her soul.

Christ demanded humility of the Canaanite woman. In response, she assumed the completely humble attitude of a beggar by acknowledging that she deserved nothing from Jesus. She did not stop begging. She continued to fervently ask and trust. Jesus was amazed and delighted by this. This woman's unusual attitude teaches us that, in every situation, even when Jesus seems to refuse to fulfill our requests and pleas, we have to hear God's knocking and to accept everything that happens as we try to open ourselves before the Lord.

TO IMITATE THE ATTITUDE OF MARY, THE BLESSED MOTHER

When the light of God's truth liberates us from the illusion of thinking positively about ourselves, and when we discover our own weakness more clearly, then remaining in God's presence can become very difficult. Without seeing any good in ourselves, we do not know what kind of attitude to assume in order to behave properly. God expects that we will stand before Him in truth and that, by acknowledging our own spiritual misery, we will trust in His mercy.

Mary, the Mother of God, is the best example for us to imitate. She completely acknowledged her own nothingness, constantly called upon God's mercy, fully trusted Him, and was unceasingly grateful for every gift: "My soul proclaims the greatness of the Lord; / . . . For he has looked upon his handmaid's lowliness" (Lk 1:46, 48). Since God looked upon the *lowliness* of Mary, perhaps in some respect she, too, felt like a spiritual beggar. The one who was exalted by God above all creatures remained before Him in an attitude full of humility.

When you discover your own spiritual misery, try to call upon Mary for help as often as possible. Without her help or intercession you will constantly be lost and you will be closed to God, who is knocking. If you see that you are unable to consent to turn your heart away from all illusions of riches so that you can become a beggar before God, then you should call upon Mary, your Mother, saying,

> You see that I waste everything. I am incapable of receiving the gift of redemption. I do not want to admit that I am like a beggar who has nothing on my own. I constantly attribute God's gifts to myself. I want to be rich before the Lord. I beg you, Mother of mercy, humble servant of the Lord, to stand before God as a beggar. Please ask Him for

mercy for me. You yourself open the door of my soul, my life, to Him.[16]

Do not be afraid. This kind of plea does not indicate your resignation. Such a plea does not mean that you are giving up. On the contrary, it is a sign that you are not giving up, even when you see your powerlessness. When you remain in the truth, Mary can allow you to become receptive to God's action and passive before your own agenda. Through her intercession, you will become like an **absorbent sponge**; you will take in graces and, thanks to this, you will be filled with God.

THE EVANGELICAL BEGGAR WHO DIES BECAUSE OF HIS LONGING FOR GOD

When you agree that you are only a beggar before God, you will gain a real chance to be united with the Lord here on earth. He, who freely accepts being stripped of all of his spiritual illusions of riches and acknowledges the truth about his condition as a beggar, seeks support in nothing besides God. Such a person turns his heart from illusions and directs it fully toward the One who is knocking. Such a person

---

[16] "Mary's maternal mediation does not obscure the unique and perfect mediation of Christ. Indeed, after calling Mary 'Mediatrix', the [Second Vatican] Council is careful to explain that this 'neither takes away anything from nor adds anything to the dignity and efficacy of Christ the one Mediator (*Lumen Gentium*, n. 62)....* Far from being an obstacle to the exercise of Christ's unique mediation, Mary instead highlights its fruitfulness and efficacy. 'The Blessed Virgin's salutary influence on men originates not in any inner necessity but in the disposition of God. It flows forth from the superabundance of the merits of Christ, rests on his mediation, depends entirely on it and draws all its power from it' (*Lumen Gentium*, n. 60)." John Paul II, General Audience on October 1, 1997, "Mary's Mediation Derives from Christ's," *L'Osservatore Romano*, English Edition (Vatican City), 8 October 1997, no. 41, p. 11.

acknowledges that all that he has is the abyss of his spiritual misery. At the moment of death, however, if the beggar calls out to God, this abyss of misery may be filled with the abyss of God's love.

To remain in this humble attitude, one must deny oneself and call upon God's mercy with the trust of an evangelical child. Upon realizing his own misery, the evangelical child believes that he will never be brushed off or pushed aside by his Father who loves him. Only great saints have such determination at the moment of their death – the moment when God exposes all of their misery to them. The Lord wants to bestow upon us the same kind of determination in awaiting the miracle of His mercy.

At the moment of death, saints, like Christ, feel as if God has abandoned them. Yet, at this moment they fervently call upon God and they die because of their longing for Him. Therefore, in a certain sense the cause of a saint's death is not only physical illness, but also spiritual hunger. They die because of their overwhelming desire to see God face to face. God wants each person to die in exactly this way. He desires that your life aim for this kind of death. God wants to lead you not only to the point where you are stripped completely, but also to the point of immeasurable, childlike trust in spite of everything.

TO BECOME POOR IN SPIRIT IN ORDER TO LIVE MORE FULLY BY THE EUCHARIST

A re you really being transformed by Christ's Redemptive Sacrifice when you participate in the Eucharist? Are you really being transformed when you receive God who offers Himself to you in Holy Communion? Does something change in your life? The elderly man, Simeon, waited his entire life for the grace to hold God in his own arms (see Lk 2:25-35). He was hungry for God. His heart was not immersed in the poisonous fumes of the temporal world. The person of Simeon symbolizes the ardor one must have while awaiting to meet with the Lord; for, it is an awaiting filled with living faith, but void of the routine that corrodes and destroys it.

If you are immersed in the temporal world and your heart finds its treasure in it, then meeting with God in the Eucharist is only an episode or a passing affect. At the same time, this meeting is also a drama that reveals the emptiness of your faith. Unlike Simeon, we are not "thirsty" for God and so we are incapable of breaking through the veil of the Eucharistic Species to encounter the Living Presence of the Redeemer on the altar. Rather, we are left to acknowledge the truth about ourselves, confess that our hands are not as pure as Mary's hands, and admit that, unlike Simeon, we do not stretch out our hands in a begging gesture toward God. Our hands are covered with the "leprosy" of sin. They look like those of a son who has strayed away from the love of his Father. Ours are the hands of a blind man who stands next to a fountain but is unable to draw water from it.

God's Divine light reveals to us the truth about our lack of awaiting to meet and to receive Him in the Eucharist. However, we should not look at this truth by ourselves; this would not be good. By knocking with His light, Jesus tells us: *Let us, you and I, look at you, whom I love, together.* Jesus desires that, upon seeing the darkness of your soul, you experience His love. He wants you to long to be united with this love in the whole truth that is revealed to you.

CHAPTER THREE

TO HUNGER FOR THE EUCHARIST

D ivine light calls out to you so that, upon acknowledging that you are closed, you, like the blind man from Jericho, will call out: "*Kyrie, eleison,*" or "Lord, have mercy on me." God wants you to try to obtain the grace of spiritual poverty by begging. By calling out to the Lord, you come closer to assuming the attitude that creates an open space for the Eucharist. Poverty is like a vacuum that waits to be filled. It hungers for the grace of forgiveness and the grace of freedom from the spiritual leprosy of sin, indifference and routine. Poverty longs to be healed of the wounds with which we, as prodigal sons, afflict ourselves when we stray far away from our Father.

God wants to give you so much through the Eucharist. His desire to bestow graces upon you, however, needs the space that is created by your interior hunger for Him. Evangelical poverty creates this space. The statement,

"Blessed are the poor in spirit," refers to those who have nothing except for God, who gives Himself over to them in the form of bread. They are blessed because the Kingdom of God, of which they become worthy thanks to the Eucharistic Sacrifice, will belong to them. They have nothing; because of this, they await the Kingdom. Consequently, the Kingdom is bestowed upon them.

God awaits each person in the Eucharist. In turn, He desires that each person await Him to the point that the attitude of awaiting becomes a growing hunger. The attitude of awaiting and the attitude of hunger coincide with each other and together they can lead to an unlimited overflow of God's mercy: "Blessed are they who hunger ... , / for they will be satisfied" (Mt 5:6).

TO THE DEGREE OF ONE'S AWAITING

During the Holy Mass, Christ gives Himself to us. He dies before our very eyes so that we may live: "Whoever eats my flesh and drinks my blood has eternal life" (Jn 6:54). The Eucharist is the source of spiritual life; it is the spiritual nourishment on the journey toward union with God. Resurrecting before our very eyes during every Holy Mass, Christ strengthens in us the hope that, upon being washed by the power of His Salvific Sacrifice, we, too, will be resurrected and transformed.

Can this inconceivable bestowal take place automatically, without our participation? God, who knocks on the doors of our hearts, does not want to impose Himself on us.

Therefore, we can receive the gift of the Eucharist only **to the degree of our interior dispositions.** By coming to the altar in the form of bread and wine,[17] Christ wants to purify us and transform us. He can do this, however, only to the extent to which we allow Him – to the extent to which we await and desire to be purified and transformed. Therefore, it is not enough to go to church in order to participate in the Holy Mass, even daily Mass. Rather, it is necessary to have an **unceasing prayer of awaiting** this meeting with Christ. Only then we can say that one lives by the Eucharist.

It is necessary for the Holy Mass to be the center of each day so that you plan the rhythm of your daily life precisely around the priority of the Eucharist. As it is with your biological rhythm, you begin the day when you wake up in the morning. In your spiritual rhythm, the beginning and the center of each day should be the Holy Mass in which you participate. The time that precedes the next Holy Mass should be pervaded by your awaiting the next Eucharist and its fruits. Even before you fall asleep, you may pray in this intention and ask for the grace to await receiving Jesus in the Holy Eucharist.

If you were to eat only once a day, then you would become hungrier by the hour. Should we not desire the Eucharistic Bread one hundred times more? Unfortunately, the Holy Eucharist is rarely associated with that which

---

[17] "By the consecration the transubstantiation of the bread and wine into the Body and Blood of Christ is brought about. Under the consecrated species of bread and wine Christ himself, living and glorious, is present in a true, real, and substantial manner: his Body and his Blood, with his soul and his divinity (cf. Council of Trent: DS 1640; 1651)." *Catechism of the Catholic Church,* 1413.

satisfies the hunger of the soul. Your daily participation in the Eucharist easily degenerates into a pious habit and routine, resulting from a commonplace schedule rather than a longing for something that constitutes the essence of life. Routine makes it extremely difficult to authentically live by the Eucharist. Does not the way that we think about the sacraments reveal how we consider them to be magical? When Christ our Lord says that whoever receives His Body and His Blood has eternal life, He is not giving a magical prescription for entering into heaven. The meaning of His words is much deeper. Habitually passive reception of Holy Communion is not enough to be saved.

In order to *have eternal life*, you have to receive the Most Sacred Body with faith. We must believe that Christ's Body is **the most important food for our souls**. When such faith manifests itself in us, then we will begin to long for the Eucharist. We will begin to desire to be united with Christ. A hunger for the Life-giving Bread will arise within us. Even more, we will also be able to satisfy this hunger at every moment because, through such arduous awaiting, our spiritual communion with Christ can take place.

We cannot be saved against our own will. Those who desire and ask for this grace and await it are saved. Even if you feel momentarily moved or touched during Holy Communion, this does not guarantee your salvation. Whoever does not await Christ, who comes to us in the Eucharist, testifies to his lack of desire to be united with Him. In fact, whoever does not await Christ, testifies to his lack of desire to be saved because salvation is precisely union with God for all eternity. Only the one who constantly awaits the Lord hidden in the form of bread, only the one who sees his salvation in Christ, can be assured that he will meet Christ at the moment of his death and will be rescued. This longing for Redemption and awaiting liberation not only for ourselves, but also for others, is the essence of living the Gospel.

During every Holy Mass, Christ knocks on the doors of our hearts so that we will let Him in and allow Him to feed us with His own Body and to immerse us in His Redemptive Sacrifice. If, however, the Holy Mass becomes a mere habit for you rather than the foundation of your interior life, then you, at least to a certain extent, reject this Most Supreme Gift. If you do not live by the prayer of awaiting the Holy Mass, then you scorn the Redemptive Sacrifice of Christ. What can be done to overcome routine? How can we live by the prayer of awaiting the Eucharist? While we await the Holy Mass, it is most important that we do not close our eyes to the truth, which the light that knocks on the doors of our souls wants to expose before us. Precisely in the brilliance of God's "knocking" light, we will gradually see the true meaning of the Eucharistic Banquet. We will discover more clearly that we ourselves are Christ's invited guests. Only when we discover this, will we await the Holy Mass with humility of heart.

THE "SICK" PERSON WHO DESIRES THE MEDICINE OF THE EUCHARIST

Awaiting the Holy Mass becomes more authentic when we discover the state of our souls in a better way and when the space of poverty created by Divine light diminishes the illusion of the good opinion that we have of ourselves. Do we really love God and desire to serve Him? If so, then why are we apprehensive to work for Him when successes cease and nobody praises or values us? Why do we feel tired so quickly? Why do we justify our decision to give up our efforts in trying to fulfill God's will by telling ourselves that we "have other, more important obligations," or that we "have our right to rest"?

If you admit to the state of your spiritual illness, which God's light reveals to you, and if you desire to remain in truth, then you will confess that in every step of your life you forget about the Lord, that you fail to live in His presence, and that your heart continuously turns away from Him. You are in love with yourself and you despise God's love. You think in a human way and pursue your own will. You are not at all interested in fulfilling the will of the Lord. Although it is very painful, this truth can generate an authentic Eucharistic hunger within you. Only a starved spiritual beggar truly awaits the Holy Mass; only a beggar desires to participate in the Banquet during which he knows he will be fed.

Your prayer of awaiting will be based solely on emotions until you acknowledge the emptiness of poverty within you. What will you do when you begin to experience the state of spiritual dryness? In this state, only the discovery of your own spiritual misery will incline you to desire to be purified and cleansed in the Blood of Christ. Initially, however, the prayer of awaiting arises from a person's shock upon seeing the state of his soul, rather than out of love for Christ. Authentic love of God is born only through suffering. Authentic love is the fruit of carrying the cross that crushes our own disorderly self-love and pride to some degree.

The Divine light of truth, by extracting even a part of your spiritual misery from the darkness of your whitewashed tomb's interior and exposing this fragment of the truth to you, will let you simultaneously see how absolutely necessary the prayer of awaiting Holy Mass is for your interior life. If you do not hunger for the Eucharist, and if you attend the Holy Mass out of mere habit instead, then this means that you do not want to be transformed by the Redemptive Sacrifice of Christ. In a certain sense, your life becomes "spiritual vegetation."

Even though the prayer of awaiting the Eucharist is necessary for the soul, it is difficult because it requires that one constantly overcome one's self and it demands spiritual effort. God sees how your capacity to do this is minimal. That is why Jesus Himself desires to await in you this Eucharistic meeting. In order to prevent your pride from being fed, however, God can hide the consciousness of this prayer from you so that you will not attribute the prayer to your ability to pray and, therefore, consider it a personal spiritual success.

Through the experience of your own spiritual misery, you can become hungrier for the Eucharist such that you desire it on the level of your will, which is the most important.

THE PRODIGAL SON'S HUNGER

The Holy Mass, also called the Eucharistic Banquet, is something like the joyous banquet that the father prepared for his prodigal son. Therefore, the prodigal son's hope-filled awaiting as he returned home to his father, staggering because of hunger and starvation, is a model for us and the way that we should await the Eucharist. When the prodigal son squandered the inheritance he had received from his father:

> ". . . a severe famine struck that country, and he found himself in dire need. So he hired himself out to one of the local citizens who sent him to his farm to tend the swine. And he longed to eat his fill of the pods on which the swine fed, but nobody gave him any. Coming to his senses he thought, 'How many of my father's hired workers have more than enough food to eat, but here am I, dying from hunger. I shall get up and go to my father and I shall say to him, "Father, I have sinned against heaven and against you. I no longer deserve to be called your son; treat me as you would treat one of your hired workers."' So he got up and went back to his father. While he was still a long way off, his father caught sight of him, and was filled with compassion. He ran to his son, embraced him and kissed him." (Lk 15:14-20)

In this parable, the son certainly left his home very rich and self-sufficient. He could afford comfortable means of transportation as well as servants. Before he wasted everything on a life of dissipation, he lived comfortably, dined well, and dressed elegantly. However, after a certain period of time, when there was not much left of his inheritance and a "severe famine struck [the] country," he was forced to sell what was left of his property and become a pauper.

When the son searched for a job, he certainly must have been dressed in rags because, if he appeared to have descended from an affluent family, then no one would have dared to offer him such a humiliating task as tending swine, since the Israelites considered taking care of impure animals disgraceful. The prodigal son's exterior appearance – emaciated, haggard, and filthy – was **a reflection of his spiritual state**. This man lived as if God did not exist. He pursued only his own will and failed to take his father's will or God's will into account.

We can imagine how the prodigal son's return to his father's home was. Now, when he made his decision to "get up and go," he was already very exhausted and weakened by starvation. He had neither money nor strength. He staggered. He was clothed in filthy rags and the path ahead of him was certainly long. How long would it take until he arrived? Days, weeks, months? Exhausted physically, psychologically and spiritually, he nevertheless walked with perseverance and persistence, renewed each day by the hope that the meeting with his father would change his life. He stumbled, fell and painfully hurt himself many times. Nevertheless, he got up and continued to walk on because he lived with the hope that he would meet with his father, and he awaited the moment when his father would embrace him.

Was not the prodigal son, in a certain way, similar in appearance to Jesus Christ, burdened with our sins, mistreated, and cruelly wounded, whom Isaiah described as: ". . . so marred was his look beyond that of man, / and his appearance beyond that of mortals" (Is 52:14)? When the prodigal son returned to the father as a beggar, his appearance was such that those whom he asked for help probably drove him away from their doorsteps as if he were a stray dog. In contrast, as soon as the father caught sight of his son, he hastily ran to him and, "filled with compassion," embraced him close to his heart. Why was the father in such a hurry? Surely the father rushed to his son because he was deeply touched. Perhaps, though, the father also rushed to his son because of his son's shocking appearance. With similar haste, our Heavenly Father comes out to meet us. He always receives us with love when, through prayer full of contrition and awaiting, we return to Jesus, who waits for us during the Holy Mass. During Holy Mass, Jesus gives Himself to us and simultaneously gives us His inheritance, which we had wasted, again.

Unfortunately, when we return to Christ, we do so only for a short time. Frequently, immediately after receiving Holy Communion, we waste this new and generously restored spiritual fortune on the most threatening prostitutes: disorderedly self-love and thinking in a human way.[18]

---

[18] According to St. Thomas Aquinas, the disordered love of self to the point of contempt of God constitutes the root of every sin. Because it makes it so man is oriented toward a temporal good, and he therefore turns his back on the eternal good. Aquinas, *Summa Theologica*, trans. Fathers of the English Dominican Province (Westminster, Md., 1981), q. 77, art. 4, 5. pp. 937-38.

No wonder it is not long before we are caught in a dramatic situation again. But when we desire to return, the Heavenly Father immediately comes out to meet us in order to immerse us once again in the Passion, death, and Resurrection of His Son. He does this not only during Holy Mass, but also when we await the Eucharist with hope and contrition because of our unfaithfulness. When we await the Eucharist, Jesus already immerses us through faith in the mystery of His Redemption. Jesus bestows graces upon us according to the degree to which we await the fruits of the Holy Mass, even if we have not yet participated in it.

THE SPIRITUAL BEGGAR'S HUNGER

The returning prodigal son resembles a beggar in a material sense because of his shabby clothing and lack of money. He is also a beggar in the spiritual sense, for he acknowledged that he sinned, he confessed his own spiritual misery, and he asked for mercy without placing conditions on his father. The prodigal son agreed to take the last place in his father's house.

When God penetrates your soul with the light of truth, you will see how much your soul is wounded, ill, and starved. You will see that you are just like the prodigal son, for whom the light of his Father's love was his only hope. You will see that just as the father bestowed his love on his son by having a feast, so, too, does God the Father desire to bestow His love upon you through the Eucharist. This light of truth will generate a deepening need within you for the prayer of awaiting the Holy Mass. Moreover, perhaps this need will grow so deep and intense that it will become the prayer of Eucharistic hunger.

Your Eucharistic hunger will intensify to the extent to which you more clearly see how dramatic your spiritual situation is. What is the point of frequently receiving Holy Communion if, upon leaving the church, you are unfaithful to God, you continue to love only yourself, and you subconsciously or even consciously live as if God does not exist? When you live as if God does not exist, you depart to that *distant country* where you waste the inheritance that you received from Him. You waste your inheritance when you think and act merely in a human way by fulfilling your own will "in the name of God." Even more, you commit adultery with idols so that your soul becomes very similar to the soul of the prodigal son and your spiritual situation resembles his dramatic situation.[19]

Perhaps it will be difficult for you to believe that, even if you live in the state of sanctifying grace, you commit venial sins as well as many infidelities. Yet, if you knew how much all of this wounds God, then you would certainly stand before Him as a spiritual pauper. Upon cooperating with

---

[19] "By reason of the spiritual union existing between Yahweh as bridegroom and Israel as a bride, the Prophets used the term adultery figuratively to designate apostasy from God or the worship of idols and Israel's infidelity to its covenant with God (Is 57:3-7; Jer 3:8-9; 5:7; 23:10; Ez 23:37,43; Jgs 2:2-13). . . . In keeping with the figurative usage of the Prophets, the disbelieving contemporaries of our Lord (Mt 12:39; 16:4; Mk 8:38), the lovers of this world (Jas 4:4), and evildoers generally (Rv 2:22) were called adulterers." *New Catholic Encyclopedia*, 1967 ed., s.v. "Adultery (In the Bible)."

God's light of truth, in a spirit of faith, try to undertake the necessary effort to acknowledge that you are a prodigal son and a spiritual beggar. When you do this you will truly begin to await your meeting with Christ in the Eucharist; you will begin to await the wonderful Banquet thrown by the Father in honor of those who are starving and in honor of those in whom He rejoices because they have returned.

When the prodigal son's father exchanged his son's beggarly garments for the finest robe and sandals, when he bestowed a ring upon him and prepared the banquet table, it was as if the son were reborn. For, the father said to his older son, ". . . we must celebrate and rejoice, because your brother was dead and has come to life again; he was lost and has been found" (Lk 15:32). The Holy Mass is the time for spiritual rebirth. If you constantly awaited the Eucharist with hope, then your evil would cease to horrify you so much and it would no longer be a cause of constant doubts, discouragement and sadness.

If you fail to await Christ's mercy, through which He desires to purify you in both the Eucharist and the Sacrament of Reconciliation, then it is not surprising that Satan offers you ever new temptations to which you succumb. You begin to ask the Lord for mercy only when your pride of perfection is wounded by your faults, which become visible to others, and the mystery of the interior of your whitewashed tomb becomes public knowledge. Is it necessary for you to wait until Christ shakes you up in this way? It is better to encounter God's love before this happens. In fact, if, upon acknowledging that there is so much misery in you that needs to be healed, you treated the Holy Mass and the Sacrament of Reconciliation differently, then God could make you a different person. If you lived with a hunger for the Eucharist, then He could infuse new life into you and change your heart so that you will not only cease wasting your life, but also draw others closer to Him.

AWAIT LIKE A LEPER

Often the Holy Scripture compares sin, which destroys the human soul, to leprosy, which disfigures and kills the body. As described in the Old Testament, God's reaction to the behavior of Aaron and Miriam demonstrates that not only mortal sin, but also thinking and acting in a human way, as well as disobedience to God's will, destroy the soul like leprosy destroys the body.

> . . . Miriam and Aaron spoke against Moses on the pretext of the marriage he had contracted with a Cushite woman. They complained, "Is it through Moses alone that the LORD speaks? Does he not speak through us also?" And the LORD heard this. . . .
>
> So angry was the LORD against them that when he departed, and the cloud withdrew from the tent, there was Miriam, a snow-white leper! When Aaron turned and saw her, a leper, "Ah, my lord!" he said to Moses, "please do not charge us with the sin that we have foolishly committed! Let her not thus be

like the stillborn babe that comes forth
from its mother's womb with its flesh half
consumed." (Num 12:1, 2, 9-12)
Miriam must have looked terrible with the flesh half consumed
like a stillborn babe! Like the prodigal son, Miriam's external
appearance was a reflection of her tragic spiritual situation.

Even though Miriam and Aaron's complaint about
Moses seems like a slight transgression, in reality it was a serious
matter. Miriam and Aaron's decision to criticize Moses, without
taking into account the circumstances that justified him, could
have destroyed the prophet's authority among the Israelites.
Because Moses was a special instrument in carrying out the
Lord's plans, Miriam and Aaron's speech, trivial as it seems,
destroyed God's action. It is similar when we think and act in a
human way. At first, it may not appear to be very evil, yet, in
doing so, we oppose God's intentions and destroy His plans.

When you look at your spiritual situation in the light
of faith, you will discover that, although in the present
moment you might not be committing any mortal sins for
which your conscience may reproach you, your soul is still
covered with the leprosy of unfaithfulness and thinking in a
human way – the **leprosy of spiritual riches.** Your soul is
destroyed by the "leprosy" of seeking your own will instead of
what God expects from you.

When you undertake some job because of God's will,
and **you burn out due to your excessive involvement,** which

71

stems from your lack of detachment from work, this too causes spiritual leprosy. You concentrate too much on the task at hand or on the goal that has been set, rather than on the Person of Jesus Christ who, by knocking on your door, asks you to allow Him to enter into the kingdom of your action. If you remembered about the Lord, who desires to enter into your emptiness, then you would invite Him into everything you undertake and you would ask Him to act through you. Perhaps, when you "work very zealously," you think that you are doing God's will. God, on the other hand, does not want you to become so involved in this way at all. Whoever gives his entire heart to a particular matter or job and forgets about God becomes like a moth that flies into a flame and is destroyed by it, rather than benefiting from the flame's warmth and light.

Our Lord desires that we try to discern His will by examining the situation, circumstances, and conditions in which we find ourselves. Certainly, when we walk in the darkness of faith, we do not always know what God's will is. Regardless, we should always seek it.

Even when Christ achieves very authentic signs through us, we still manage to forget about Him. By this attitude we cause others to close themselves off to the Lord and we destroy God's action. Our spiritual leprosy can then infect those around us and will be reflected in the spiritual lives of those with whom we have come in contact.

God's action through us does not have to reflect the degree of our union with Christ at all. Jesus' sharp words remind us of this: "Many will say to me on that day, 'Lord, Lord, did we not prophesy in your name? [...] Did we not do mighty deeds in your name?' Then I will declare to them solemnly, 'I never knew you. Depart from me, you evildoers'" (Mt 7:22-23). Even if your life is full of miracles, if you are infected with the leprosy of evil, then you limit the explosion of God's mercy. Even more, you are accountable for doing this.

When we discover how the leprosy of thinking in a human way destroys our interior life, even if this leprosy is intertwined with the good that God accomplishes through us, we will begin to await the Eucharist or confession as the time during which we may be purified of leprosy. This is how the lepers from the Gospel awaited their encounter with Jesus. They awaited their encounter with Christ because they knew that He was their only hope since leprosy was an incurable disease at that time.

Except for God's mercy, is there any other cure for the leprosy that destroys our souls? Imagine that a person who is dying from cancer finds out that an extraordinarily effective cure has been found. Would this person not do everything in his power to obtain this medicine and to take it regularly? Would it be possible for this person to ignore such news or to forget to take the medicine? If someone is unaware about the state of his soul and fools himself thinking that he is healthy, then such a person will not ask for a cure. Only the person who, thanks to God's light, sees

73

the leprosy that destroys his soul and asks to be rescued can be purified.

The prayer of awaiting the Eucharist is the supplication that allows you to be constantly immersed in the graces of Redemption and cleansed of the leprosy of unfaithfulness. All of your illnesses are nothing in the face of God's infinite mercy, which overflows into your heart when you beg for it: "In my misfortune I called, the LORD heard and saved me from all distress" (Ps 34:7).

Each time something of the mystery of the whitewashed tomb is exposed before you or when, in God's light, you see that you are still immersed in your daily sins, try to immediately free yourself from these sins, to be purified, and to be reborn. In fact, it is sufficient to call for mercy – to ask to be immersed in the fruits of the Most Holy Sacrifice. So little is necessary. For example, you can look at the Crucifix and ask interiorly:

> Lord, purify me of the leprosy of my sins.
> Purify me of the impurities of my adultery with this
>   new idol.
> Immerse me in Your death and Resurrection.
> Restore in me the dignity of being Your child.

Then you can also immediately thank Him for already doing this.

Is there a forgotten Crucifix hanging on your wall, covered with dust? The Crucifix is not just an ordinary object. Rather, it is the sign of Someone who loves you and desires to save you at every moment of your life. How often do you adore the Crucifix? Try to gaze at it like the leper who gazed at Jesus when His purifying hands touched him.

Every form of prayer, every moment we stand before God with faith and allow the light of truth to penetrate us and His mercy to touch us, can be a source of purification. Every time your heart turns away from the idols of this world and wants to cling to the heart of Jesus, you are purified. You are also immersed in the waves of mercy when you joyfully call upon God, "Abba, Father!" (Gal 4:6) and are grateful that, by His Sacrifice, Jesus obtained for you the right to be a child of the Heavenly Father. Why, therefore, do you so rarely ask to be purified of the leprosy of sin?

Perhaps one day, you will see your pride and your bad will, which cause you to constantly forget about the prayer of awaiting the Eucharist. In fact, is your neglect not a symptom of extreme stupidity? If you do not desire to be purified, it is as if you reject salvation. Each time you see your unfaithfulness but fail to ask to be purified by the power of the Most Sacred Sacrifice you destroy yourself and, even more, you damage your relationship with God. In this way, you are then like a leper who knows that Christ can heal him. However, upon seeing Christ pass by, the leper does not want to go out to meet Christ. Instead, he tells himself, "I will not ask for healing. I prefer that my body decay." It is unbelievable that human pride can reach such a degree.

Surely, saints consider themselves as the most infectious lepers. They, however, are the ones who ask God for mercy most frequently. They live each day so as to await the Eucharist. When they die, they also long to be immersed and purified once more in Christ's Sacrifice.

Christ cannot leave the prayer of a person who hungers for the Eucharist and humbly awaits the fruits of Holy Mass unanswered. We can be sure that torrents of graces will be poured upon such a person and that he will be cleansed from his leprosy; for, such a person responds to the Lord's bidding: ". . . ask and you will receive; seek and you will find; knock and the door will be opened to you" (Lk 11:9). This is why saints do not need to go to Purgatory, and the gates of Heaven are immediately opened before them.

ASK MARY TO AWAIT FOR YOU

Nothing compares to the purifying and healing action of the Eucharist. There is no other cure like it for our spiritual diseases. When you await the fruits of the Holy Mass you are already purified to a certain extent because you meet with the Eucharistic Christ through faith and hope.

When you pray in the morning and in the evening, during adoration and during meditation, and during your prayer immediately before the Holy Mass, you can always ask God for the grace to await the Eucharist. In fact, nothing is more important than being open to the grace of Redemption. This holds true for you and for all of those for whom you pray.

At the beginning of the day, during your morning prayer, you can entrust yourself to Jesus, through Mary. During this time, you may ask Mary herself to immerse you in the Redemptive Sacrifice of her Son. If you see that you lack good will and you do not want to live by the Eucharist, ask Mary to await the Holy Mass in you, ask her to thirst and quest for the Lord in you, and ask her to live with a hunger for God according to the example of her Son. Ask her to pray for mercy for you and for all those you entrust to God.[20] If you do not ask for her intercession, then how can she help you? She does not want to take away your freedom.

The Mother of God is the one who knows best how desperately you need to live by awaiting the Holy Mass. She also knows how you damage your relationship with God by lacking this attitude. The more often you ask to be immersed in the Most Holy Sacrifice, the more you will be opened to the action of grace and the more you will be obedient to God's will. This, in turn, will make you a more effective instrument in the Lord's hands; you will become a sign of hope for a world immersed in sin.

---

[20] Cf. John Paul II, "Mary's Mediation Derives from Christ's"; Cf. Second Vatican Council, Dogmatic Constitution of the Church *Lumen Gentium*, trans N.C.W.C. (Boston, MA: Pauline Books and Media, 1998), no. 62.

CHAPTER FOUR

LIVING BY THE MYSTERY OF THE EUCHARIST

W hen we adore creation instead of adoring God, we become blind to the Lord's light and deaf to the Lord's calling. Just as the evangelical blind man from the Gospel did, we should ask the Lord:

> Lord, make me see. Enlighten the eyes of my soul with Your light, by which You knock on the door of my heart.

This light is grace that wants to embrace you, move you, and draw you closer to the Lord. It also wants to heal and transform you so that, in its splendor, you can look at the world as if through the eyes of God.

In this extraordinary light, we can see Christ as the Lord of the world as well as infinite love. Divine light wants to show us the face of the Lord, who was crucified for each one of us and who offers Himself daily in the Eucharist. The Lord's light will allow us to be immersed in Christ's death and Resurrection during the Most Holy Sacrifice. In addition, it will also prolong the action of the Most Holy Sacrifice throughout our entire lives. In this way, our lives can gradually be unceasingly immersed in the Lord, who died and rose for us.

When we live by the mystery of the Eucharist in this way, we will die to ourselves. The old persons in us will gradually die. Yet, through the immersion in the Resurrection of Jesus Christ, the new person will be born according to the example of the One who loves us to the end and expresses this love most profoundly in the mystery of the Eucharist.

OUR PARTICIPATION IN CHRIST'S SACRIFICE

The Holy Mass is the center of our spiritual life, the answer to all of the questions and doubts that torment us. It is the rescue from our afflictions and difficulties. It is the perfect cure for every evil.

The real and effective actualization of the one and only Redemptive Sacrifice is the source and summit of interior life. It is also the beginning, means and goal of interior life. Therefore, each of us, as a disciple of Christ, should be fully open to this great mystery. Together with the priest who celebrates the Holy Mass, we participate in the unique Priesthood of Christ, who offers Himself to the Father as the Priest and, at the same time, as the Sacrificial Victim. Therefore, not only the priest, but we too have a share in celebrating the Eucharist when we offer our lives and our very selves in a special way, together with the Sacrifice of the Lord's Body, to the Father.[21] If we do not participate in the Eucharist properly, then we cannot fulfill the mission to which God calls us as His disciples.

The Church stresses that, during the mystery of faith, we cannot be like foreign and silent spectators; rather, we have to learn to offer ourselves as a sacrifice, as we, along with the priest and through his hands, offer the Host.[22] Just as Christ offers Himself to the Father, we, united with Him, have to give ourselves over to the Father. With Christ, we have to entrust our wills to God, and give Him the right to arrange our lives as He pleases. In this way, we unite ourselves with the essence of Christ's offering about which St. Paul writes: "For this reason, when [Jesus] came into the world, he said: / 'Sacrifice and offering you did not desire, / but a body you prepared for me; / holocausts and sin offerings you took no delight in. / Then I said, "As is written of me in the scroll, Behold, I come to do your will, O God"''" / (Heb 10:5-7). We have to strive to assume this attitude of self-relinquishment during the Holy Mass. Because of this attitude, union with Christ, the Great High Priest and the Sacrificial Victim, can become the very essence of our lives, both during the Eucharist and in day-to-day events. Yet, this sacrificial attitude is very difficult to assume during Holy Mass. This is the precise reason why the Church very realistically says that

---

[21] Dogmatic Constitution, *Lumen Gentium*, nos. 10, 34.

[22] Walter M. Abbott, ed., "Constitution on the Sacred Liturgy *Sacrosanctum Concilium*" in *The Documents of Vatican II*, trans. directed by Joseph Gallagher (NY: Herder & Herder, 1966), no. 48.

at first we have to learn this attitude.[23] We must learn it, however, in communion with Christ. Moreover, to learn this attitude is not about a single act of will or a momentary ardor; rather, it is a lifelong process of living in deeper communion with the Redeemer.

THE ATTITUDE OF CONTRITION AND POVERTY DURING THE EUCHARIST

Contrition, or humbly acknowledging one's own evil while trustfully awaiting God's mercy, is the attitude that makes it possible for us to properly participate in the Most Holy Sacrifice of Christ, which is actualized during Holy Mass. Indeed, from the very beginning of the Eucharistic Liturgy, the Church exhorts us to reflect on our spiritual misery when the priest says, "My brothers and sisters, to prepare ourselves to celebrate the sacred mysteries, let us call to mind our sins."[24] Therefore, we have to acknowledge that we are sinners and stand in truth before God.

The words of the Liturgy of the Holy Mass constantly remind us about the attitude of contrition. Immediately after the Act of Penitence we pray the words of the blind beggar from Jericho, "*Kyrie, eleison*," or "Lord, have mercy" (ibid., 674-75). The *Gloria*, also, reminds us that Christ, the Lamb of God, "take[s] away the sin of the world" and it contains the plea "have mercy on us" (ibid., 679). This plea is simulta-

---

[23] Ibid.

[24] James Socías, "The Celebration of the Mass," in *Daily Roman Missal*, 6th ed. (Chicago, IL: Midwest Theological Forum, 2004), 673, hereafter cited in text.

neously an acknowledgement that we have participated in the sin of the world as well as a plea for God's mercy, which is our only chance for salvation.

The Liturgy of the Word frequently speaks about sin, calls us to penance and assures us of God's forgiveness for those who are contrite and fulfill His will. The silent prayer that the priest says to himself before the proclamation of the Gospel is full of contrition: "Almighty God, cleanse my heart and my lips that I may worthily proclaim your gospel" (ibid., 683). These words simultaneously express the awareness of one's own unworthiness and the conviction that one needs to be prepared by God's divine and purifying action to participate in the Holy Mysteries. In addition, after reading the Gospel, the priest kisses the Book and says silently to himself, "May the words of the gospel wipe away our sins" (ibid.). In this way, the priest expresses faith in the fact that the Word of God has the power to wipe away guilt and to cleanse man interiorly. Moreover, once he prepares the gifts, the priest bows profoundly over the altar and quietly asks that the Lord God ". . . receive us and be pleased with the sacrifice we offer [Him] with humble and contrite hearts" (ibid., 691). Finally, the awareness of one's unworthiness and the desire to be purified is eloquently expressed when the priest washes his hands and quietly utters, "Lord, wash away my iniquity; cleanse me from my sin" (ibid.).

Consciousness of one's own misery, and calling upon God's mercy by trustfully pleading for forgiveness, appear in the texts of the liturgical prayers. Before receiving Holy

Communion, we pray with the words of the Lord's Prayer, "... forgive us our trespasses as we forgive those who trespass against us" (ibid., 793). Subsequently, we plead for peace and beg that God grant us this peace and that He "Look not on our sins, but on the faith of [His] Church" (ibid., 795). The acclamation, "Lamb of God, you take away the sins of the world," reveals to us Christ the Lord and the source of God's mercy for a world for whose sin He offered His life as a sacrifice (ibid., 797). Finally, immediately before receiving the Lord's Body, we acknowledge, "Lord, I am not worthy," and we confess that we believe that only one of His words is sufficient to heal us (ibid., 799). Are all of these words that we say during Holy Mass, however, truly alive in us? In reality we frequently, if not always, repeat these words and fail to truly believe in our hearts what we say with our lips. This attitude damages our relationship with Jesus.

God Himself is the One who comes out to meet us, His disciples, in order to give us the grace to participate in the extraordinary mystery of the Eucharist. Yet, we respond to Him in a routine way that, sometimes unconsciously, demonstrates some form of our indifference. When we realize more deeply how lukewarm our response to God's invitation to the Eucharistic Banquet is, we will begin to see more clearly the reality of our sin about which St. Paul speaks. Therefore, should we not acknowledge that we are "sold into slavery to sin" (Rom 7:14)? Should we not admit that, by our own strength, we are incapable of fulfilling our vocation as Christ's disciples? The best thing to do is to admit to our incapacity in advance and acknowledge that, without Jesus and His special mercy, we would certainly waste our participation in the Holy Mass.

God's Word becomes alive only in the humble and poor soul that is docile to His action. Let us try to make a space of poverty in our hearts. Let us try to prepare a place for Jesus so that He Himself can participate in the Eucharist for us.

It is highly recommendable that we come to Holy Mass and attempt to acknowledge as deeply as we can, in accordance with the Penitential Rite, that we are sinners. Upon seeing your helplessness, trustfully call out to the Giver of everything to rescue you. He wants to do all things for you because He loves you and He sees that you cannot live without His love. When you contritely stand before God and see that you are incapable of participating in the Holy Mass with deep faith, Jesus Himself will participate in this great mystery with faith because He lives in you. Jesus listens to the words of the Gospel and responds to the exhortations of the priest. He listens to the holy words of consecration and receives the blessing that He wants to bestow upon you through the priest. **Although you are a sinner, you will become like a vessel filled with God.**

LIVING DAILY BY THE EUCHARIST

The *great mystery of faith* that we ponder during Holy Mass is the foundation of all of our interior lives. That is why we must try to live by the Eucharist in our daily lives rather than limit ourselves to living by the Eucharist only during the Liturgy. Living by the Eucharist in our daily lives means to be open to everything that we experience during the Liturgy and to assume this attitude of openness in the concrete realities of our everyday lives. It is important not to divide up our day in such a way as to dedicate one hour to God and then the rest of the day to the temporal world.

By offering ourselves as a sacrifice to God during Holy Mass, we give our Lord the right to constantly and freely do what He pleases with what we offer to Him. In the attitude of spiritual poverty, by dispossessing ourselves and by trying to lovingly and submissively accept everything that He Himself desires to give us as alms, we can **give ourselves over to God's disposition.**

If extended beyond the time of the Holy Mass and into our daily lives, identification of ourselves with Christ's Sacrifice means to give up our own rights and freedoms. It means to attempt to accept everything, but especially those things which are contrary and disagreeable to our nature. In this way, together with Christ, we will be able to give to the Father an offering from our lives. The prayer that concludes the Spiritual Exercises of St. Ignatius of Loyola expresses this attitude of being entirely at God's disposal: "Take, Lord, and receive all my liberty, my memory, my intellect, and all my will – all that I have and possess. Thou gavest it to me: to Thee, Lord, I return it! All is Thine, dispose of it according to all Thy will. Give me Thy love and grace, for this is enough for me."[25] This prayer concisely expresses the spirit of true offering and total bestowing. Such a prayer conveys the Christian attitude that is closely united with the attitude of Christ's complete poverty and sacrifice. Such an attitude communicates the true gift of one's self and the conscious agreement to allow God to be in control of one's life and to direct it. The sincere Christian attitude entails giving up a life that is organized according to one's own desires and ideas – a life that does not count on God and on His will.

The Church encourages each one of us to assume the attitude of acknowledging our evil and awaiting God's mercy during the Liturgy of the Eucharist. To live daily by the Most Holy Sacrifice, we should assume this attitude as often as possible in our everyday activities and work. Precisely in this **attitude of contrition**, we have the possibility to open ourselves up to the Lord, who speaks to us not only during the Eucharistic celebration, but also in every moment of our lives.

During the Holy Mass, God speaks to us through the readings and the liturgical texts. In addition, we can listen attentively to His Word after we leave the church, whether through prayerful reading of the Holy Scriptures, or by opening ourselves up to a **dialogue with God** as He speaks to us through our daily lives, people, events and situations. Each moment of our lives is rich in grace. In every minute God desires to convey something to us just like He does during the Eucharist.

---

[25] Ignatius of Loyola, *The Spiritual Exercises of St. Ignatius of Loyola*, trans. Father Elder Mullen (NY: P.J. Kenedy & Sons, 1914), published as PDF-document by ixtmedia.com, http://www.jesuit.org/images/ docs/915dWg.pdf.

Holy Communion, which we receive in a sacramental way during Holy Mass, is a call for us to aspire to live in **communion with Jesus** also in our daily lives. Our communion with Jesus is communion between a contrite sinner and his Redeemer. The contrite sinner is the one who acknowledges his own evil and trustfully stretches out his hands toward the Redeemer. Jesus, Our Redeemer, forgives the sinner for everything, immerses him in His Redemptive Sacrifice, and purifies him. We have to give ourselves to Christ, whose Body we receive during Holy Communion, in order for Him to be alive within us. This means that we must give Him our bodies and souls so that He may use us and make Himself present through us in the world. Only then can we bring Him to all those who are in need and share with them the gifts that we have received from the Lord.

At Mass, we pray together with God's people gathered in the church. After the Liturgy ends, we should continue to live in unity with the community. Living by the Eucharist in our daily lives signifies **unity with the Church community,** which is expressed, not only in our prayer, but also in our daily attitude.

During the Holy Mass, when we profess our faith through the recitation of the Nicene Creed, we open ourselves up to the fullness of God's revelation, and we confirm that we have chosen God. In fact, the Lord also expects the **profession of faith** from us in our daily lives. Maybe we will not necessarily pronounce our faith directly with words, but we certainly should express it in the attitude we assume in the presence of those with whom we come in contact, whether at home or at work.

Just as we bring our intentions for our brothers and sisters to God during the Prayer of the Faithful, so too, should we try to assume this **attitude of mutual responsibility for the Church** and God's people in our daily lives. We should take care of individual members of the Mystical Body of Christ. Practically speaking, this usually takes place in the context of the family, the domestic Church. Living by the Eucharist in our daily lives means to take care of the faith of every member of our family, as well as to develop the life of faith at our parish.

At the end of Holy Mass, we are sent forth with an invitation to **spread the Good News** wherever we go in such a way that everything that happened during the Eucharist will become alive to those, both the faithful and unfaithful, whom we come in contact with throughout the day.

Even if we know very well that everything that takes place during the Holy Mass should be continuously actualized in our lives, it is still very difficult for us to live daily by the Eucharist. Our rescue is our calling out to Jesus and asking that He Himself live and act in us. Just as we are to be open to His action within us during the Liturgy of the Holy Mass, so too, should we make room for Him in our hearts so that He can live out the Eucharistic mystery in us in our daily lives. By living out the Eucharistic mystery in us, Jesus will make us more disposed to God. With contrition,

He Himself will carry on a dialogue with the Father in us amid the events of our daily lives. He Himself will be open in us to communion of life with the Father. Jesus will live in us in unity with the Church community. He will take care of our domestic Church. He will be an apostle to others. He Himself will live in us with the certainty of faith that we are redeemed as sinners. Finally, He will receive God present in every person we meet and in the events and situations in which we are placed daily.

Christ Himself will unite your life with the Sacrifice offered on the altar so that it may become an offering to your brethren. You yourself will see that everything good that happens in your life is not yours; rather, it is His work. Therefore, in your heart, the space of poverty will deepen. As a result, Christ will be able to act in you so that the fruit of the Redemptive Sacrifice can be realized more and more perfectly in your life.

TO BECOME POOR IN SPIRIT IN ORDER TO FULFILL GOD'S WILL

Human nature, wounded by original sin, is oriented not toward God, but toward the affirmation of one's own *I*. When our *I* is threatened, our wills create vast networks of defense mechanisms, most often subconscious, in order for our *egos* to maintain their positions. However, self-containment is not enough. For, when threats to our egos diminish, our wills make attempts to expand our *egos'* territories, and as if to infinitely widen their borders. The human heart longs for transcendence. But unfortunately, we opt for false transcendence.

By knocking on your door with His light, God wants to direct your desires and open you to the only true transcendence – Himself. When God does this, it is as if He is telling you:

> Give to Me your will and its unceasing desire to go beyond itself and follow after a false light. This path leads nowhere. It can lead to your damnation.

The desire to expand the territory of one's own *I* is dangerous, not only for the soul, but also for the psyche. Quite often this desire is the source of disappointment, wounds, and illnesses. God invites you to give up this desire and to become poorer in spirit, more and more emptied of yourself. Only then will the desire to fulfill God's will appear in you in place of your false longings.

Poverty means to be stripped of your own desires so that the infinite will of God might reign in you. Only God's will can fulfill the longings of the human heart, which is lost, saturated, and wounded by its harmful desires. In essence, the hidden and subconscious goal of all of our desires is God Himself: "You made us for yourself" says St. Augustine.[26] And so, we can attain self-realization only by uniting ourselves with the loving will of God.

---

[26] Augustine, *Confessions*, bk. 1, no. 1, p. 21.

CHAPTER FIVE

THE MIRAGE OF THE HUMAN WILL

"What do you possess that you have not received?" (1 Cor 4:7) asked St. Paul. If we receive everything from God, then we owe everything to Him. Everything is a gratuitous gift from God. Each gift calls for gratitude.

Our wills, which are wounded by original sin, want to be grateful to themselves as much as possible and grateful to God as little as possible. This tendency present deep within our souls strengthens our conviction that we are *someone*, that we have something of a creator in us, that we can manage on our own without the One who created and redeemed us. The consciousness of having something on our own that is ours tempts us because it pleases our self-love. It is so pleasant to be somebody great, to be able to give something to ourselves and to others. The more we think that we possess something by ourselves, the less we need God and His bestowing will.

The splendid mirages of riches, which seem to us to be such reliable sources of support, function only for a time. At a certain moment, seeing that illusory supports can possibly wound or even destroy us, our Lord God shines His light on the deceitful character of these illusions. When something comes crashing down because of your resistance to God's call, and when you distressfully look at the debris of your illusions, it is difficult to believe that God is enlightening you. But He will not abandon you. The same Divine light will point out to you that to see the debris of illusions is a gift. You will begin to be grateful because you will discover that you have been rescued just in this way.

THE ILLUSORY NATURE OF SUPPORTS OTHER THAN GOD

Our desire to find support in this world is not only directed toward different matters and things, but also toward people such as our family members, friends and dear ones. Attachment to people pertains not so much to the individuals themselves, but rather to the images we hold of those individuals. Our egoism concocts these images to fulfill its "needs." We surround ourselves with false images of other people and these images create our illusory riches. These illusory riches are like a **world of cardboard masks** that prevent our contact with the real persons and, even worse, separate us from God's light.

God, who knocks on the borders of the world of our mirages, desires to unmask the falseness of these mirages. Only when we respond to God's grace and allow Him to unmask our illusions, and only when we question our illusions regarding other people, will we be capable of loving others or receiving their love. A person who agrees to lose his illusions becomes poorer in the evangelical sense. As a result, the emptiness of spiritual poverty appears within him, and it is into this space that he can invite God. In this way, the world of cardboard masks, which our egoism wants to continuously dominate, begins to change into a kingdom of which God is the only ruling Lord. Until you really rely on God, you will never love with the kind of love to which Jesus invites you, "I give you a new commandment: love one another. As I have loved you, so you also should love one another" (Jn 13:34).

If a man who does not rely on God wants to find support only in his wife, then is he able to fully love her? Egotistic expectations and desires that someone will satisfy another person's most hidden dreams and needs arise within each person who seeks support in another human. Can a husband who is enslaved by these types of expectations see the face of Christ in his wife? Can a husband see the One who desires something completely different than what he himself desires? A husband, who is dazzled by the false image of his wife and by the **mirage** that tells him that she is supposed to fulfill his expectations and needs, becomes blind and deaf to the knocking of God's light. Such a man is unable to fulfill God's will with regard to his wife.

The same, however, holds true for the wife. Will she see the real needs of Christ in her husband if, instead of relying on God, she continuously tries to lean on some ideal, yet completely false image of her husband? In reality, such a woman does not love her husband; rather, she loves only herself. Distorted self-love is the true motive for her actions.[27] One can say that the riches of human desires put the factory of countless mirages, false ideas, and illusory images of others into motion. This goes against the attitude of spiritual poverty within the marital relationship and closes off the world of human love to the Lord's knocking. In addition, this remains true for all of our relationships with other people, including relationships with children. If you seek reliance in your child, if you count on him to reciprocate your love and to fulfill your hopes and dreams, then you will become enslaved by these expectations. If you seek reliance in God's will and not in the false image of your son or daughter, then you will be able to see what Christ, who is hidden in your child, desires. You will be able to bestow gifts upon your child and to receive various gifts from him in accordance with God's will.

When you want to rely on persons or things, without relating them to God, then you stop seeking God's will. Put

---

[27] According to St. Thomas Aquinas, the disordered love of self to the point of contempt of God constitutes the root of every sin. Because it makes it so man is oriented toward a temporal good, and he therefore turns his back on the eternal good. Cf. Aquinas, *Summa Theologica*, trans. Fathers of the English Dominican Province (Westminster, MD, 1981), q. 77, art. 4, 5. pp. 937-38.

in another way, you barricade yourself within the illusory territory of your own *ego* and fortify its borders against God, even though He wants to lead you by the light of His will and bestow His love upon you.

When you experience difficulties, you lose a sense of security. In turn, anguish overcomes you. Therefore, you should always seek reliance in God's will. By seeking reliance in God's will, you will cease to feel estranged and isolated. In addition, you will stop fearing people and circumstances. You will cease to be excessively preoccupied with what other people think about you. Peace will begin to reign in your heart – a peace that comes only when you seek to rely on God and follow His light. In His love and from the Cross, Jesus granted you the grace to learn God's will and to fulfill it so that you, too, could repeat after Him: *My food is to do My Father's will* (cf. Jn 4:34).

WHEN YOU TURN THE FULFILLMENT OF GOD'S WILL AGAINST HIM

The danger of seeking reliance in things other than God threatens every aspect of our lives, even that which we do because it is God's will. Through different trials of faith, our Lord frequently questions the illusory hopes that we place in the fruits that come from fulfilling His will.

If you seek to rely on your success, even success that results from fulfilling God's will, then you will have to taste the bitterness of failure. Failures humble our prideful desire to appropriate God's gifts. They make us poorer. Failures question our illusory conviction that, upon fulfilling God's will in a specific matter, we can relax with the blessed awareness that we are finally in order before the Lord. A person who is poor in spirit never rests in this illusion. He needs God in every moment and he sees no other rescue apart from God. Regardless of whether or not he succeeds or fails, someone who is poor in spirit places his hope only in God. Such a person knows that he is a useless servant (cf. Lk 17:10) who neither wants to do anything useful nor wants to lean on any of the fruits of his own works. He is characterized as persevering and patient. He **awaits that which he does not deserve.** This is why a person who is poor in spirit leans only on God, who loves him, even though his hands are always empty before God. Unfortunately, we will not have this kind of attitude until we are saints. Because we are wretched, even when carrying out God's will, we do not rely on God alone. Instead, we lean on that which we do because it is God's will. We constantly attempt to prove to Him that something belongs to us.

When you make an important life-changing decision – for example, you change jobs, establish your own company, or build a new house – you frequently ask yourself, "What is God's will?" and you try to act in accordance with it. Despite this, you easily feel self-assured as your new company progresses or the walls of your house go up. Even before you know it, you start to think that you are now "somebody." You become rich without God. In doing so, you build the kind of edifice of spiritual riches in your heart about which Jesus Christ severely remarked, "woe to you who are rich!" (Lk 6:24).

Someone who is poor in spirit seeks only God and His will and desires no other riches. God comes to those who have nothing because only those who have nothing truly need Him. Thus, it is written that theirs is the kingdom of heaven (cf. Mt 5:3). However, everything on which we count and in which we place our hope apart from God, even if it is something we are involved in because of God's will, is a barrier that separates us from the Lord. It is a "treasure" that occupies the place in our souls that should be empty for the Lord who knocks.

Spiritual riches are not only an obstacle in seeking God; they are also a mirage, an illusion. Ultimately, all of our various material, intellectual, and even spiritual "treasures" can instantly become useless. If you build a comfortable house for yourself, how do you know that you will live in it, even if you build it because of God's will? What if you suddenly have to travel to another place? What if you die before the job is finished?

For the person who attempts to live an interior life, not only material goods, but also spiritual goods constitute an important reliance. For example, perhaps you are taken by some excerpt from Sacred Scripture and you hope that this excerpt will deepen your spiritual life. In this way, the excerpt becomes your treasure. Why do you assume that this

Scripture excerpt is meant for you in particular? God's plan can be quite different. Perhaps you are simply supposed to relay this pertinent excerpt to someone else for whom these particular words will happen to be very important. Meanwhile, your life will not change at all. Do not place your hope in any religious practices or in any words because, in doing so, you witness to the fact that you **disregard God** and do not want to lean on Him. You live as if He does not exist.[28]

If you strive for the attitude of spiritual poverty in fulfilling God's will, and if you do not try to create riches out of the fruits of God's will, then you do not have to be stripped. However, by leaning on persons or things, you sentence yourself to the torment of being stripped. When the Lord God sees how His gifts that you appropriate wound you and close you to His love, He intervenes with His light of truth. He does this in order to show you that these are only deceiving mirages, which His power can instantly dispel.

If you count on gifts and place your hope in them, then you lack the wisdom of faith. Even worse, you ignore God. In some sense, you even despise God. If you disregard the Lord of the Universe, and you do not want to lean on Him, then you live as if He does not exist.[29] When it all

---

[28] "St. Thérèse had no difficulty in recalling texts and passages . . . When I told her that I should like to be able to do that, too, but my memory was not good, she answered: 'There you go again, desiring riches and possessions! To lean on these things is like leaning on a piece of red hot iron; it will always leave its little scar. We must lean on *nothing*, even in the case of those things which we have reason to believe might help us in the spiritual life.'" Geneviève, *Memoir of My Sister*, 32-3.
[29] Cf. John Paul II, Apostolic Exhortation, Reconciliation and Penance *Reconciliatio et Paenitentia*, (Boston, MA: Pauline Books & Media, n.d.), no.18; Cf. *Catechism*, no. 2113.

comes down to it, who is God for you, especially if you do not lean on Him, even when fulfilling His will? If a human friendship conceals God from you, then you will have to be deprived of that friendship. If you rely on money, then the Lord will have to strip you precisely of money. When you hope in your work, then you will either lose your job or cease to hold the position to which you are attached. In addition, you may experience so many work-related failures and difficulties that work becomes a source of torment for you rather than your primary source of satisfaction. All of this happens because, rather than allowing God to be the foundation, you allow whatever you do or possess because it is His will to be the foundation of your joy and hope. This happens because you build a barricade with God's gifts – a barricade that closes off the access through which His grace comes into your life.

When you discover how much you ignore and despise the Lord, remember that, despite everything, He never stops loving you. He loves you precisely as you are: as someone attached to your idols, as someone who lives as if He does not exist, and as someone who turns even that which you do because of His will against Him. He never stops loving you even though you continuously reject Him and wound Him by turning your heart away from Him and by seeking reliance in your own riches.

God unceasingly fights so that you will finally understand that **He alone and His holy will are your only true reliance.** Once you realize this, then you will really begin to live according to the words that are repeated daily in the Lord's Prayer: *Fiat voluntas Tua – Thy will be done.*

OUR *FIAT*

For what do we really live? Do we live to eat, drink, and die? Is life all about spending time in an increasingly more pleasant way while we are healthy, only to grow old and die in tremendous pain and suffering as the majority of people do in the end? What is the purpose of our lives? Is it to have a comfortable standard of living in this world? The Lord God created us so that we would live according to His image and likeness. Is it real when we please our own *egos* by professing the principle: *My will be done?* Professing the principle *my will be done* is an extreme symptom of egoism. In addition, it is contrary to the attitude of someone who is poor in spirit, who acknowledges his total dependence on God, and who does not desire to realize any of his own plans that may contradict God's will.

Attachment to our own wills leads to unnecessary suffering, to the destruction of whatever we touch and whatever we do. This is the fundamental cause of our troubles and suffering. It is also the cause of the painful wounds that we inflict not only upon ourselves and others, but also, and especially, upon Jesus. All evil in our lives is born of the rejection of the words: *Your will be done.* No supernatural good can come from our opposition to God's will. Supernatural good arises only when we are submissive to the Almighty's will and plans. If a person flees from God's will and fulfills his own, then he cannot be God's instrument. Instead, he chooses to be his own god. As a result, he despises the Only God.

Unfortunately, whether visible or hidden, your motto is: *my will be done.* In your relationship with God, do you not behave like Aladdin sometimes? Aladdin discovered the magic lamp that gave him special control over a powerful genie. He only had to rub his lamp and immediately the genie appeared before him. After bowing before Aladdin, the genie awaited Aladdin's orders. You, too, have a magic lamp, otherwise known as your own way with God. In other words, you call upon the Lord of the Universe and place before Him matters which He "must" attend to and arrange, such as an important exam, an attractive trip, or the "solution" to financial difficulties. Sometimes, somewhere near the end of your list, you add: *Your will be done.* However, is there not some hidden perversity present in this way of thinking? Although you do not say outright to God, "You have to do this or that," your behavior indicates that you think that you know very well what is best for you. Someone who is "spiritually educated" such as yourself is aware that he cannot impose things on God. Therefore, you discreetly remind the Lord of your merits. Meager merits? Yes, very meager. Nevertheless, through your attitude you hold your "merits" before God and say, "You know, Lord Jesus, how You should settle this matter for me."

Living according to the principle *my will be done* means treating the Lord God as if He were the genie in the magic lamp, as if He were our servant and our slave. Even though Jesus Christ was the One who became a servant of men and even though He accepted death on the Cross for us, He still calls us to imitate His poverty, His humility and His hunger for His Father's will. He desires that we strip ourselves of our own will and be ready to question all of our plans.

The path of spiritual poverty consists of repeatedly making attempts to live according to the words "not my will but yours be done" (Lk 22:42). Therefore, perhaps you have to agree to fail an exam, even though passing is so important to you. You must agree to fail, even if by failing you will not get to go where you want to go, or you will not receive the increase in your pension that you want. Perhaps nothing will come of your plans. Perhaps God's plans will be realized instead. What if God wants you to go abroad, but His plan is for you to depart later than you desire? What if He has some plan related to your travels – a plan of which you are still unaware? What if, by failing your exam, you are saved from serious danger to your soul, a danger that would have threatened you had you not failed the exam? Do not reject that which has been prepared for you by the One who loves. Do not refuse the will of the One who wants to give you everything that is best – best, however, in the broader scope of your entire life. This perspective keeps in mind that which is most important.

Because God keeps in mind the scope of your entire life, it is good that He crucifies your own plans if they are not according to His will. If He wanted you to lose everything and everybody, just like Job, then so be it because this is precisely what is best for you (see Job). Nothing and no one can give you riches as great as the gifts that God prepares for you. Spiritual poverty creates in our hearts the space of freedom in which it is possible to receive God's gifts. This light of poverty shows us that the riches of human desires are a mirage or an illusion that not only disappoints us, but also separates us from the Lord.

Christ says, ". . . my yoke is easy, and my burden light" (Mt 11:30). We can experience this when we follow the rule: Your will be done. If we follow this rule, then our lives will become much easier and simpler. After all, in the Creator's initial plan, He desired to make man happy. Adam and Eve lacked nothing until they opposed God's will. In opposing God's will, they brought upon themselves the tragedy in whose consequences we participate today. If someone asks you how he should behave in order to obtain true happiness, then you can simply respond: *Your will be done, God.* These words point out the path that leads to eternal happiness. These words are our road signs toward the heavenly homeland. Man's tragedy, however, lies in the fact that he does not trust the Lord and rejects His will. Namely, man avoids God's will in order to fulfill his own will. By so doing, he sentences himself to torment, which our good Father did not intend for him. Such torment is the consequence of his opposition to God's designs. Transgressing God's plans always makes our situations worse; we multiply our suffering and inflict pain on others.

Even if we intellectually accept that God's will is the best, we often strive to convince not only ourselves and others, but also God Himself, that our own wants coincide with His will. Because God respects our freedom and our choices, we can impose our desires upon God and compel Him to change His holy plans. The Lord consents to this even though each modification of His will means only greater suffering for us. If, for example, someone who is called to consecrate his life to the Lord God through priesthood or religious life rejects this vocation, then God will permit this person's decision and provide another solution, another path to holiness, such as in marriage. This path, however, will be more difficult and longer because it is not according to the initial, merciful plan of God. On this path there is a multitude of unnecessary torment, suffering and pain because God's initial plan was different, better, and gentler. Therefore, for someone who opposes God's will, the burden becomes heavier and the yoke becomes bitterer. The only way to improve the situation is to return as soon as possible to fulfilling God's will on this new path of life. Even if a person willingly crucified God's initial plans, His new plan can become that which is the best and the easiest. Some additional and unnecessary suffering that cannot be avoided will remain: the consequences of despising God and His will.

It is important to accept this suffering in the spirit of humility. The best thing to do is to ask Mary to receive it. When she humbly accepts any kind of suffering for us, our yoke becomes easy and our burden light again. Is it possible for a person who is very weak and fragile to live by his own strength according to the words: *fiat voluntas Tua*? If you see how being obedient to God's will is difficult for you, then you can ask Mary to live in obedience to God's will in you. After all, she was the first to fully and perfectly utter *fiat* to God. She alone repeatedly gave that *fiat* for her entire life. Mary is our Mother. God gives her to us as a special help. We need to be open to this gift, to take advantage of it by allowing the Blessed Mother to fully live in us according to the words: *fiat voluntas Tua*.

CHAPTER SIX

TO WORK AS IF NOT WORKING

Our entire lives usually take place between home and work. In these two worlds we are frequently as if different persons. Looking in the light of faith, a place of employment is like a true pantheon of different idols. These idols express not only our needs and desires but also our fears and reservations in relation to jealousy, rivalry and the desire to make money. It is so difficult to seek God and His will in this dense jungle of matters, problems, and aspirations. Nevertheless, this work has been given to us for a reason: so that we learn how to carry out God's will and try, in accordance with His will, to be detached from everything that we do in order to become poor in spirit.

Through dramatic events, or even through a lack of events, the Lord God continuously knocks on the door of the territory of your work and your vineyard, which is supposed to become the Lord's vineyard. In the presence or absence of dramatic events, God attempts to show you how important it is to maintain a proper distance from that which you do. Distance is another definition for spiritual poverty. Our Lord God is interested in the freedom of your heart, in the interior silence where you can listen to even the subtlest of God's words. He is interested in interior silence, which will also calm your tense nerves and free you from anxiety, stress, and facial wrinkles. According to St. Paul, who emphasized the insignificance and transience of temporality, you must act as if not acting, work as if not working (cf. 1 Cor 7:29-31). Everything you have, that you greedily hold on to, or that you long to acquire, is like sand that slips between your fingers.

Christ the Lord said, "Unless you turn and become like children, you will not enter the kingdom of heaven" (Mt 18:3). When we work, we are to be like children who are unfamiliar with ideas such as carrying out tasks. Little children are unaware of the burden of responsibility. Rather, they simply play because Mom wants them to play. At every moment, they are ready to interrupt their play, if Mom says so, and without any regret, knock down their sand castles in one fell swoop.

CHASING AFTER THE GOLDEN BOWL

God wants to use your work, the people with whom you come in contact at work, and the difficulties that arise during work, as instruments in forming your soul. A large part of your adult life is spent at work and this time should serve you on your path to sanctity. If you look at your job without faith, then you shut God out of an important part of your life. When you are excessively absorbed in what you do, you behave as if you have forgotten that you are God's child and that you have an immortal soul, which your Heavenly Father wants to feed with His love, even when you are at work. There is a saying, "a person digs his own grave with his teeth," because he does not feed himself properly. In your interior life, you do likewise. If you fill your soul at work with aspirations and desires that come from your lowest instincts, then you feed it with garbage, which is like poison.

So frequently we are like pagans at work. We do not give honor to the true God. Instead we honor various idols, such as greed, egoism, and human regard. Wanting to please those on whom our position and salary depend, very often we are unscrupulously ready to betray God and our interior lives; we are ready to sell our birthright for the proverbial "lentil stew" (see Gen 25:29-34). In other words, preoccupied with pursuing our careers or our "holy peace," we crucify Christ and, without taking into account how we treat Christ, we reject Him who always loves us. We chase after mirages like madmen, and we jeopardize our souls. A very old, evocative painting depicting Satan as he stands on the top of a mountain, holding a glowing golden bowl in his hands, recalls our frenzy. The bowl's deceptive brightness draws large crowds that run recklessly toward it. The people do not notice, however, that the abyss of hell stands between them and the object of their desire.

The golden bowl of career, money, or power always glows in an equally deceptive way. St. Thérèse warned one of her sisters: "You give yourself up too much to what you are doing, as though each duty were your last and that you were hoping that you had finally reached the end."[30] The Lord wants you to work for Him, not some gain or peace of mind. If you looked at your work in the light of faith, then perhaps you will discover the emptiness and nonsense of each of your actions that are not oriented toward God.

THE DANGER OF SUCCESS

Constant work-related success can turn out to be dangerous for our interior lives. Work-related achievements constitute a type of riches that strengthen our illusions of self-sufficiency and close our hearts to God. We are convinced that our success is the fruit of our own efforts and capabilities. We see no need for God's intervention in work-related matters. As long as we manage well on our own, we do not see the need to open the world of work to the Divine light, knocking on our doors.

If work becomes a goal in itself and you undertake it, not because of God, but only to affirm your self-worth, then you turn your work life into an illusory fortress for your pride, a stronghold against God. In addition, when you live for work, you also waste a good portion of your life and fail to take advantage of the graces obtained for you by Christ on the Cross.

---

[30] Geneviève, *Memoir of My Sister*, 33.

God desires that your work also help in your conversion. He desires that your work transform you. If God wants to lead you to Himself along the path of poverty, then He will also submit this realm of your life to the trial of purifications. When you experience failures at work, you will discover that you cannot manage without God. Perhaps, only then, will you begin to really pray.

The experience of helplessness can help you to discover that your only chance is to call upon the Lord for mercy through the prayer of someone who is *poor in spirit* – someone who knows that he is nothing and is capable of nothing on his own. God does not want us to complete our tasks and work perfectly at the expense of our interior lives. Strengthening our good self-image is destructive to our interior lives. It is against the attitude of spiritual poverty. Only when our helplessness manifests itself and the reality that we are unable to fulfill what God expects from us rises to the surface, will our opinions of ourselves slowly begin to change. Only then, will they be more truthful. Through trials of faith at work, **God can demolish the edifice of our spiritual riches** and gradually form the attitude of poverty within us. When God begins to purify our approach to work in this way, we will not be so concerned about our professional status, our personal development, or the success of our new qualifications. During the period of purification, these types of values cease to seduce us.

A different, supernatural motivation to work arises according to the depth of the development of your interior life.

As this supernatural motivation surfaces, you will become more detached from your own plans and poorer in your ambitions. When making specific decisions, you will ask more frequently for God's will before all else. You will start to interpret the experiences with which you are confronted at work differently. You will discover trials of faith in these experiences.

THE DISTANCE OF SPIRITUAL POVERTY

When you start to look at work in the light of faith, you will discover that everything good in your life, including your work-related achievements, is God's property, not yours. "What do you possess that you have not received?" (1 Cor 4:7), asks St. Paul. Perhaps you are convinced that these words pertain to everything except your success at work?

Someone who is poor in spirit stands before God in truth and does not hide behind the masks of perfection and self-sufficiency. He believes that God loves him just as he is. Consequently, he is willing to admit to his limitations, fallibility, weaknesses, and misery, even in matters pertaining to work.

Spiritual poverty also pertains to such matters as your initial opinions regarding a particular topic, your specific ways of problem-solving, or your unique style of being when you are at work. If you consent to God's action, then the Lord can begin to deprive you of the false riches of illusions through various experiences or through the interior light of truth. He can deprive you of your illusions that you are a good worker or a superb specialist who is capable of arranging everything as you please at a moment's notice by your own skills or experiences. You will see that, if you are creative and endure in your work, have interesting ideas, or can direct others, then it is because God wants to accomplish this good through you.

God desires that you become poor in spirit in your professional life. He wants you to experience that you are unable to be faithful to Him on your own, even for one instant. It might not be easy to see that the desire to complete your work well, even if it is no longer caused by egoistic motivations but by the desire to fulfill God's will, arises within you as a result of the action of His grace. Thanks to God's light, you may surprisingly see that you work well, even though laziness or the prideful seeking of your own glory through work formerly governed you.

You should try to maintain the distance of spiritual poverty, not only in relation to the tasks at hand, but also in relation to your superiors and your subordinates. Do not be swept off your feet by compliments used to entice you to work. Do not succumb to the illusion that you can do anything on your own. Sustaining such illusions is contrary to the attitude of spiritual poverty. If God bestows upon you the graces you need in order to work, and this only fills you with pride, then you destroy your spiritual life. Perhaps, sometimes you become tired of difficult experiences at work and, by succumbing to the temptation of rebellion, you conclude that the interior life is a luxury that you cannot afford. You rationalize and tell yourself, "After all, I have a family to take care of and I must get down to business instead of wasting my time in prayer." This type of "solution" is a fatal illusion fabricated by pride, which is exacerbated by the lack of success to which it was accustomed. Moreover, these illusions have fatal consequences. Do you really think that you can handle your own problems without God's help?

If you continuously encounter new problems at work, then it is a sign that you appropriated God's gifts. God has to purify you because you are prideful. Your failures are reminders that you lack the attitude of someone who is poor in spirit. If you lack this attitude, then the Lord has to repeatedly foil the realization of your plans or the recommendations of your superiors. In addition, He will permit you to be helpless in the sense that, despite your efforts, you will be unable to prove yourself. Only then will you see more clearly how bent you are on success. You will realize how much you desire and need success, even if you delude yourself into thinking that you have already passed through this phase of spiritual life.

Furthermore, you will be convinced of how many desires you have – desires that are so far from the attitude of poverty, such as the eternal dream of being *somebody*, of gaining recognition, and of showing-off in front of others or, at least, in front of yourself. Why are you so surprised that the Lord God does not want to fulfill all of your dreams? You must be sanctified through your work, which means that you should not build a chapel for your *ego*. Here, too, the Lord knocks on the door and asks for His place. The only answer that He expects from you is the distance of spiritual poverty. The distance of someone who is poor in spirit allows him to see that, upon dedicating his heart to work, he turns work into an idol and, therefore, wounds the Only God.

The extent to which you discover your wretchedness more clearly is the extent to which you also experience that you are completely helpless in relation to it. You will experience that you cannot change your approach to work. You constantly seek to assert your own self-worth; you appropriate gifts that God bestows upon you; and, in reality, you do not want to fulfill God's will. Such consciousness can enable you to begin to see that your only chance to be rescued is in an unceasing plea for mercy.

The person who is poor in spirit – who has nothing – places all of his hope in the Lord. He does not depend on any of his talents or capabilities. When you stand before God with this attitude, He will surely look upon your lowliness (cf. Lk 1:48), and He Himself will begin to cast your idols from their pedestals. Through your work, He will bestow upon you that which He Himself wants. At that time, the stress and the tension that accompany your work will diminish and you will joyfully and peacefully attend to your tasks like a child who is always secure at the feet of the Heavenly Father.

GOD IS CONCERNED ABOUT YOU, NOT ABOUT YOUR ACHIEVEMENTS

God desires that you experience each work day as if it were the last day of your life. Naturally, this does not mean that you should feel excused from planning professional matters. You should plan, but do not be excessively attached to the idea that you will fulfill these plans yourself. What if God's designs for you are different?

The most important desire for you should be that your work is according to God's will. If you attempt to remember that each work day could be your last, then you will seek God's will with greater intensity and you will try to carry it out more faithfully. When you try to look at your work while keeping in mind that you will die, then you will understand that you cannot afford to waste one-third of your life on something that will turn out to be of no value when you die. At the moment of death, neither your professional achievements nor qualifications will count. How many university degrees you earned or how many languages you know will not be important, if, in the end, all of it did not draw you closer to God. You have to carry out your work in the best way, but only so that you can express your love to God by being obedient to His will. That being the case, work will become for you a path to holiness.

If God allows you to be successful, then this is good. However, if He desires to purify you from your pride by allowing you to fail so that you can become more humble, then this is also good. The important thing is that your soul is docile to this transformation so that through your work-related experiences a new person can be born within you. This new person will stand before God with empty hands at the moment of your death and say:

Lord, You see that I did nothing good in my life on my own, but I believe that You love me.

If you work, keeping in mind that you must show God obedience and faithfulness, then you will be free when the day of your death comes. You will not be bothered by matters that you have no time to fulfill. You will not worry how others will manage without you. All of these things will not enslave you because you will know that you are replaceable. By being aware of this when you are involved in work, you will cease to appropriate fruits that the Heavenly Father constantly bestows upon you. Furthermore, you will see that work is not your final goal. Something else really matters. God desires that, through your work, you be open to Him. He desires **that you give yourself as an offering to Him**. You must live by the desire to unite yourself with the Lord. Your work should serve this purpose as well.

Do not be discouraged by the difficulties and trials of faith through which you pass. Our Heavenly Father is the One who gives these to you and He loves you. **For God, you are what matters, not your achievements**. He desires not only to take care of you, but also to fill you with Himself. When stripped of all the delusions pertaining to who you are, you will begin to rely exclusively on faith that God loves you gratuitously, for nothing. Then you will embark on the path of one who is poor in spirit according to the first beatitude – the path toward union with the Lord God in love.

CHAPTER SEVEN

TRIALS OF FAITH ON THE WAY OF GOD'S WILL

O ur faith can be very shallow – so shallow that the peace that flows from it becomes insidiously dangerous because it lulls us to sleep. Shallow and stagnant faith resembles the surface of a pond on the top of which accumulate layers of decay. It is not enough to go by boat and systematically cleanse the surface of the water of the muck that grows on it; rather, it is necessary to get to the root of the problem, to the deepest part of the pond, in order to discover the source of contamination. From where does it come?

It is absolutely necessary for God's light to penetrate deep into the pond, down to the sediment, so that the source of the problem emerges, surfaces, and discloses its hideous appearance. God is the One who knocks in this strange way in order to shake up the shallowness and exteriority of your routine faith. The discovery of this decaying or contaminated source may shock you because it is the image of your inner-self, of what is inside of you, and of the world that you conjure up in your own imagination. There is no need to be afraid; these are only trials of faith through which God questions your delusional peace. These meandering trials of faith may be numerous and varied. They may unexpectedly change course and be illuminated by either a stronger or weaker beam of God's light.

You will never be alone during times of trial because you are incapable of discerning God's will if He is not already with you, accompanying you, and lighting your path on these extraordinary quests. The action of God is like a combination or mixture of light and shadow. Therefore, His light can sometimes be veiled and seem as if it has gone out. Yet, the sun always shines, even if it is covered by clouds and appears not to exist at all.

THE TIGHTROPE OF GOD'S WILL

To love God means to unceasingly choose His will. This demands constant concentration and steadfast effort. It is comparable to walking on a tightrope. This concentration and effort has to be all the more intense because the tightrope of God's will is suspended over an abyss, the dangerous abyss of self-will, which contradicts God.

When walking on the tightrope of God's will, you have to be alert and step ever so carefully. You do that which God expects of you only if you complete the steps on this tightrope. Each false step denotes a fall into the abyss of self-will.

The tightrope of God's will is not a typical line like you might have seen in the center of a circus tent. You are not alone when you walk on it. You meet various people and things. You solve problems and encounter everything that life brings your way. If, for example, you discover that you have a musical talent, then you may encounter a piano on the tightrope of God's will. Be careful. Even though God certainly wants you to take advantage of your talent, you should still take a good look at this instrument first. Look and see how this instrument is attached to the line of God's will in such a way that you cannot lean on it. The rope's strength is such that you can play the piano, but you cannot lean on it. If you try to lean on it, then you and the piano will fall into the abyss. For a person who desires to fulfill God's will, even if the person has undisputable musical talent, the music can never be a goal in and of itself. In this sense, music cannot become the only support. This person must live for God, not for music.

You are only a human, and your body has its needs. While walking on the tightrope of God's will, you often encounter a table that is set for a meal. Be careful. Take a good look at the table. Is the table not fastened to the tightrope like the piano? If you seek above all your own pleasure when eating, instead of seeking God's will, then you try to lean on the table and you can fall into the abyss.

People who you encounter on your way along the tightrope will pose a similar dilemma. They also walk very gingerly on the tightrope and take careful steps. Do not try to lean on them because you will lose your balance and fall off together. You will encounter the needs of your neighbors, your spouse, your children, or your parents. God, however, does not want you to be rich by relying on them. God's will is your only reliance. Only when you open the world of your relationships with others to God's light, will you serve Christ in others rather than serving their egoism.

The tightrope of God's will also runs through the workplace. You must be alert and careful there too, by stepping in such a way that you do not fall. God expects you to work diligently and honestly. He does not want work to become a source of reliance for you. He expects that, when faced with different tasks, you maintain a certain distance of spiritual poverty.

The tightrope of God's will pertains to all aspects and levels of your life, including all your conceptions and visions, even your vision of the path to holiness and your image of God. You should not rely on your own vision of God's will either because, if you do, then you will fall into the abyss of your own will. Finding yourself in this abyss is always something fatal.

DIFFICULTIES IN INTERPRETING GOD'S WILL

Recognizing the direction of the tightrope of God's will is not always easy. Sometimes a flash of God's light reveals only a small segment of the tightrope, while up ahead there is only darkness, which makes the path seem as if it has been abruptly cut short. Even though you try to peer with your eyes of faith and although you can see that the line appears again in the distance, you can only see the abyss directly in front of you. Is this a trial of faith in which you cannot discern God's will? What should you do? Standing on the visible part of the line of God's will, you should carefully and with particular concentration feel for the line with your foot, even though you cannot see it. God's will must be sought with determination. God desires that you exert a lot of effort in this respect. When you put forth this effort, He will surely allow you to discover the direction of the line with your foot as the line extends further into the darkness. He will allow you to find and feel and understand His will. It does not matter if someone who is looking from the other side and sees how gingerly you walk in the shadows, thinks that you are walking on air and that you will fall at anytime. Other people might think that you are crazy. You, however, will know that you are relying on God's will.

In order to walk on this invisible tightrope, you cannot lose faith that it exists. Only faith can protect you from falling into the abyss of your own will as you proceed into the darkness. When walking on the tightrope of God's will, you may come to a point where the darkness will be so dense that you will cease to see the line at all. It will be completely useless for you to attempt to patiently feel around with your foot in order to detect God's will. The Lord will make it impossible to feel or understand it. You can become impatient when your mind and experience also stop helping you. In this situation, God expects you to be crazy and leap into the darkness. After all, it is not an ordinary line. The line of God's will may abruptly break off and reappear somewhere else two stories below. The most important thing, though, is that you have within you **the desire to seek the will of the Lord**. Only then will you decide to jump, even though by doing so, you may experience a violent fear, as if you suddenly fell down a stairway. This fall does not have to be great, but you will think that you are falling into the abyss where you will vanish and die. To your surprise, though, you will land safely and God will allow you to quickly discover His will anew.

Such difficult trials of faith are made up of new situations in your life – situations in which God expects you to seek His will in darkness. Perhaps one day you will unexpectedly lose your job or your means of survival. Perhaps you will fail an important exam, or someone dear to you will leave you. In such moments, you will feel helpless and will not know what you are supposed to do. All of your self-certainty will disappear. You will not be able to delude yourself into believing that you control everything in your life. You will be afraid, but you will gain the chance to rely on God in your poverty. The Lord expects you to trust Him in such situations and to leap into the abyss of uncertainty. Do not be afraid. He will intervene; He will sustain you and give you everything that you need. Your loving Father, who allows you to experience a trial of faith, never wants to wound you or do something bad to you. He only wants to disturb the satisfied part of your shallow faith, so that a real hunger for His will can be born within you – the hunger of someone who is poor in spirit and sees that the problems in front of him are beyond his power and capabilities to handle.

Whether you see it or not, the line of God's will always exists. Sometimes it may be thin like a strand of hair, giving you the impression that it could instantly break. You may then be afraid of perishing and falling into the abyss after taking the next step. In these situations, God wants to reveal to you that you cannot lean on your own feelings or experiences, your own reason or mind. Through deepened poverty in feeling or understanding what He is doing with you, the Lord wants your hunger to fulfill His will to increase. What if this tightrope seems to be as thin as a thread, and your reason and experience tell you that it cannot withstand the weight of your body? In the end, you still walk without falling. In such moments, God Himself upholds you; His loving hands lead you so that you will experience that your only reliance is in Him and, at the same time, in His will.

When walking on the line of God's will and, with determination, seeking the direction in which He leads you, you must be led **by the spirit** of God's promptings and **not by the letter**. If you are touched by Jesus' words, "If anyone wants to go to law with you over your tunic, hand him your cloak as well" (Mt 5:40), you still are not always able to literally follow the indication. St. Thérèse of the Child Jesus comments that "It is not always possible in Carmel to practice the words of the Gospel according to the letter. One is obliged at times to refuse a service because of one's duties; but when charity has buried its roots deeply within the soul, it shows itself externally. There is such a delightful way of refusing what cannot be given that the refusal gives as much pleasure as the gift itself."[31]

Something similar happens in our lives. In many instances, we often have to refuse someone because fulfilling the request would not be in accordance with God's will. This happens, for example, when parents cannot always fulfill all the wishes of their children. There are many such situations wherein someone asks you for some kind of "cloak" and you cannot give it to him because it is necessary for you to fulfill God's will. In all these situations, we have to ask what the Lord expects from us.

Similarly, we have to understand Christ's words, "Should anyone press you into service for one mile, go with him for two miles" (Mt 5:41), according to the spirit and not the letter. These words do not indicate that you have to always change direction as often as someone tries to persuade you to join him and to walk with him on the tightrope of God's will. Rather, you must ask the Lord what He expects from you in each concrete situation. In order for you to say "no," humility and trust are required. Sometimes it is easier

---

[31] Thérèse of Lisieux, *Story of a Soul: The Autobiography of St. Thérèse of Lisieux*, 3rd ed. trans. John Clarke (Washington, DC: ICS Publications, 1996), 228. Translation of *Histoire d'une âme: manuscrits autobiographiques (Editions du Cerf and Desclée de Brouer*, 1972) Citation is from Manuscript C, 18r°, addressed to Mother Marie De Gonzague–Ed.

to say "yes," which you utter for the sake of peace of mind. However, following the spirit and not the letter of God's commands, you cannot go to the other extreme and seek to justify your *ego*. You should not be concerned with proving to yourself and to others that you cannot give over anything, because often it is God's will that we possess certain things.

With an awareness of your own powerlessness and with the attitude of someone who is poor in spirit, it is important that you trustfully stretch out your hands to God and beg Him for His light. To be liberated from a subjective view when trying to determine or discern what God's will is in your life, your cooperation with a regular confessor is very helpful.

THE TRAP OF PHARISEE-ISM

When following the tightrope of God's will, you may experience at a certain moment that you are beginning to feel more and more sure and stable. You may think to yourself that, in the end, it is possible to learn something as difficult as walking stably on a tightrope. When you stand without shaking and when you are less tense, you know that you are walking in the right direction.

Maybe, because of God's will, you are able to fulfill some sort of function that is a source of joy for you. Maybe you complete a project that gives you authentic satisfaction. Maybe you have built a house or established a family in accordance with God's will, such that now you are finally docked at your own quiet port. All of these accomplishments may lead you to feel quite rich before the Lord, and the deadly layer of decay will begin to grow on your faith.

In every aspect of your life, even those things that you do because it is God's will that you do them, you are in danger of seeking reliance apart from God. When you do this, **your own vision of God's will** may manifest itself and it will become your riches. Even if you do not fully realize it, you stop aspiring to assuming the attitude of spiritual poverty and seeking reliance in God. Your own vision of God's will is the only important thing to you; it is what you want to rely on and it is that to which you become increasingly attached. The unique source of security and joy that you find is no longer in God. Instead, your security and joy are in what you do, because it is God's will. In this way, you turn against God, disrespect Him, and show Him contempt. Even though it seems like you are walking on the tightrope of God's will, you use it to your own ends to fortify your pride.

When you begin to realize your perverseness, you may become terrified. For example, under the pretext of fulfilling God's will, you hold Him in contempt more than someone who does not believe in Him. It is as if you pretend to be someone who is poor in spirit for whom his only treasure is to fulfill God's will. However, in reality, you secretly attribute to yourself that which the Lord accomplishes through you. Upon this you build your own illusory riches. In this way, do you not become a conniving thief of God's treasure? When the light of God reveals this truth about you, then you will begin to understand that unless you convert from your sinful ways, your life will be more and more deeply immersed in evil, and you will stray away from God. You will discover that although you see your evil, you still pursue it.

Is it not true that God has the right to take away the life of a person who has such an attitude at any moment? Would it not be an expression of His mercy? Such an act of mercy would end the person's life at the best moment – the moment when there is still a chance for the person to be saved. Therefore, what can you do in order to turn back and walk away from this path leading to damnation? Prayer and openness to God's mercy are necessary. The prayer of someone who turns the fulfillment of God's will against his own Lord, however, is the prayer of a Pharisee. In addition, the efficacy of the Pharisee's prayer – the prayer of a person who is closed to God and His will – is limited. When someone lives as if God does not exist, his prayer is not in a position to change him because it cannot open him to the renewing action of the Holy Spirit. Understanding and acceptance of Christ's testament spoken from the Cross, "'Woman, behold, your son.' Then he said to the disciple, 'Behold, your mother'" (Jn 19:26-27), is the rescue in this situation. If you accept the testament Christ gave while dying on the Cross, then you will know where to find your rescue. Christ gives you Mary as your Mother. Ask Mary to intercede for you. Ask Mary to extend her hand to you. Ask Mary to lead you across the tightrope of God's will, according to His desires. Tell her:

> *Mary, please ask God for me, a sinner. On my own, I am incapable of rising above that which enslaves me. I even turn the fulfillment of God's will against Him. In my Pharisee-ism, I am always closed to Him. I ask you to intercede on my behalf, so that I may attain the miracle of a transformed heart. I do not have to see this transformation, but I do ask for it. Please beseech and grant me the grace of mercy. Also, pray for all of those who, like me, are entangled in the spirit of this world and for all those who are closed to the Lord and His healing light.*

It is necessary for you to ask Mary as often as possible for Her intercession. She, your Mother, intercedes for you, even when you do not ask her to do so. But, when you do ask her, when you give her your consent – your "yes," it is as if her hands are freed. When you entrust yourself to her, she can obtain everything from God. She can even ask for a miracle, such that you will begin to be poor in spirit, as someone who lives with the hunger for God and His holy will.

CHAPTER EIGHT

TOWARD COMMUNION WITH GOD'S WILL

God enlightens you by knocking on the door of your heart. His light, however, is the Divine light. Therefore, if His light shone fully, it could blind you. But this light is the light of mercy that desires to draw you in by the gentleness of its promptings, instead of paralyzing you by its power. Do not force God to paralyze you with His light like He did with Saul just outside of Damascus (cf. Acts 9:3). The Lord encourages you to gradually open yourself to an increasing sensitivity of conscience. He desires that your conscience constantly and attentively listen to His call so that you may perceive even the slightest expressions of His calling presence.

Each successive grace that you receive will lead you to a greater sensitivity to God's promptings. In turn, these promptings will become quieter and gentler like the tiny whisper of the wind that the prophet Elijah encountered when he stood at the entrance of the cave where he awaited the Lord (cf. 1 Kings 19:12).

Our Lord is a jealous God. He is not content with ordinary awaiting. He is only content with the awaiting of someone who is poor in spirit, of someone who has nothing on his own. Because of his attitude, this person's entire being expresses a hunger for God's coming and his thirst for God's holy will. Such thirst recalls the scenario wherein a traveler is dying to drink even one drop of water as he struggles to survive in the desert. In response to such severe thirst, God is willing to bestow upon the soul that for which it desperately longs.

DEAD LIKE A BRICK

The Holy Spirit breathes wherever He wants. Jesus referred to this in His conversation with Nicodemus. When responding to Nicodemus' doubts as to whether one can be born again, Jesus replied: "The wind blows where it wills, and you can hear the sound it makes, but you do not know where it comes from or where it goes; so it is with everyone who is born of the Spirit" (Jn 3:8). Through various signs of His action, you will register the Holy Spirit's presence in your life, but you will not know from where it comes or to where it wants to lead you. Jesus spoke to Nicodemus about the new birth that is supposed to help you to fully open yourself up to God. This birth is supposed to make you more sensitive to the working of the Holy Spirit.

By taking a closer look at your life, you will see how strongly you resist grace. Quite often you want so much to understand and know everything in your spiritual life. At the same time, you want to impose your own will and your own concept of your life on God. You lack the attitude of spiritual poverty. As a result, you not only strive to track the mysterious ways of the Holy Spirit, but also seize His power and use the Divine Wind for the purpose of pushing your own chariot.

You are not submissive to the quiet promptings of the Holy Spirit; you are immobile like a brick that, despite the wind, stays put. A person who concentrates on himself and is full of his own plans becomes very slothful with regard to the Holy Spirit. Such an individual resembles a heavy brick – a lifeless and closed object that is very difficult to move from one place to the other. Such a person actually senses the wind, but the wind does not do him any good since he has made up his mind to stick to his own plan of action. When you are like a brick, you cease to be poor in spirit. You take care of yourself, make plans, and try to resolve your problems as if God does not exist. You are incapable of responding to the winds of the Holy Spirit, of cooperating with His grace, and of fulfilling His will.

God does not want to leave you alone in this state, like a brick, subjected to your own fate. When you are resistant and closed to His delicate knocking, God is ready not only to pound on your world so aggressively that everything is shaken to the core, but also to come like a hurricane that is capable of tossing even the heaviest bricks into the air. When He comes to you in this way, you will discover how much you mean to God and what kind of power He uses to win you over. Such a storm, however, can devastate its surroundings. A hurricane that moves bricks can also completely destroy an entire house. God can allow these situations to occur in order to convert someone. Such situations occur in the lives of the saints. This all happens so that one person can be more open to fulfilling God's will and can be sanctified.

God causes great devastation now and then. He only does so, however, because He knows that, later, the holiness of the person in whose life He permitted the devastation will result in corrective graces. These graces will be outpoured through him not only on those who experienced the effects of the devastation, but also on countless others whom the person, himself, will never know.

TOO PERFECT TO FOLLOW CHRIST

We are not sure if the evangelical rich young man belonged to the Pharisaic sect. He definitely was almost perfect. Apparently, however, he was dissatisfied with this, since he ran to Jesus one day and, throwing himself at Jesus' knees, asked Him, "Good teacher, what must I do to inherit eternal life?" (Mk 10:17). Jesus must have been a noted authority for the rich young man. Christ must have been Someone great and important, since the rich young man knelt before Him and asked Him the most important question of his life. In response, Christ reminded the rich young man about the commandments. When He learned that his listener had fulfilled all of the commandments from his youth, Jesus did not express any reservation. Instead, He simply looked upon the rich young man with love.

Most likely, the rich young man was extraordinarily faithful to the decrees of the law. Therefore, Jesus said, "You are lacking in one thing. Go, sell what you have, and give it to [the] poor and you will have treasure in heaven; then come, follow me" (Mk 10:21). First the **loving gaze** and then Jesus' call to be united in a special way with God were gusts of the Holy Spirit, who desires to give new direction to a person's life. How did this young man respond to Christ's call? How did this "perfect" young man respond? St. Mark the Evangelist noted that the young man's face fell upon hearing these words and that he left sad because he had many possessions (cf. Mk 10:22). Is it not strange that a person becomes sad because of the loving gaze of God Himself? It happened, even though the rich young man was perfect like a new, expensive, and meticulously polished marble lid of a whitewashed tomb.

Perhaps the young man was so perfect that he became not only materially rich, but spiritually rich as well. Perhaps he felt like the lord and owner not only of many earthly *possessions*, but also of **spiritual goods**, which made him somebody great according to his own thinking. When the rich young man met the Lord of all goods and saw his inability to fulfill Jesus' call, *he left sad*. Burdened with the wealth of exterior and interior riches, the rich young man resembled a heavy brick more than a light balloon that is free to be carried by the winds of the Holy Spirit. How such riches can close a person toward God's call! The rich young man did not resemble a mere brick. Rather, he resembled a beautiful block of tediously polished marble. He is the image of a soul who rejects God's knocking, is unresponsive to God's call, and remains closed like a whitewashed tomb.

The rich young man lacked the attitude of Mary who perfectly responded to the *loving gaze* of God by becoming His handmaid, attributing nothing to herself, and agreeing that nothing belonged to her. Only someone who is poor in spirit realizes that he possesses nothing. Everything that he has at his disposal, he has because of grace. Even when he is the owner or the steward of great benefits, he does not consider himself to be the master of them. Such a person realizes that goods do not belong to him and that he can be deprived of them at any moment. Thanks to this attitude, these things become neither his riches nor the weight that pulls him down toward the earth and makes it impossible for him to be submissive to the promptings of God's will.

We have to defend ourselves against spiritual riches because they can lead us into a situation similar to that of the rich young man from St. Mark's Gospel. We are capable of despising God's love and fail to submit ourselves to the promptings of the Holy Spirit, who desires to lead us to salvation. What is the use of our burdensome or excessive external perfection?

LIKE A BALLOON CARRIED BY THE WINDS OF THE HOLY SPIRIT

The new birth, about which Jesus told Nicodemus, can cause you to become fully open to God. Only when you are fully open to God will you be sensitive to His bidding like a light and free balloon carried away by the wind. You will be responsive to the Holy Spirit because you will be poor in spirit. A balloon does not know where the wind comes from, or where it goes. Therefore, it is completely submissive to the wind's action and becomes like a playful slave of the wind. A person who is open to God, and born again, should be submissive to His will like a balloon is submissive to the wind.

When you become poor in spirit, you will stop analyzing the situations in which you find yourself and it will not be necessary for you to understand everything. Of course, you will not stop reflecting on some things, but you will analyze them only reservedly. Therefore, try not to focus on understanding where the wind of the Holy Spirit is blowing or to where it is leading you. Instead, focus more on how to be a faithful servant of this Divine Wind, how to be submissive to every prompting of the Holy Spirit, and how to await everything that He wants to do with you, regardless of where it leads.

ZACCHAEUS' FOLLY

St. Luke's Gospel contains a good example of someone who was as dead as a brick for many years – immersed in his own sinfulness – and yet, upon being called by God, abandoned all of his attachments and allowed himself to be snatched away by the winds of the Holy Spirit. This person is the tax collector, Zacchaeus:

> Zacchaeus . . . was seeking to see who Jesus was; but he could not see him because of the crowd, for he was short in stature. So he ran ahead and climbed a sycamore tree in order to see Jesus, who was about to pass that way. When he reached the place, Jesus looked up and said to him, "Zacchaeus, come down quickly, for today I must stay at your house." And he came down quickly and received him with joy. When they all saw this, they began to grumble, saying, "He has gone to stay at the house of a sinner." But, Zacchaeus stood there and said to the Lord, "Behold, half of my possessions, Lord, I shall give to the poor, and if I have extorted anything from anyone I shall repay it four times over." And Jesus said to him, "Today salvation has come to this house because this man too is a descendent of Abraham. For the Son of Man came to *seek* and to save what was *lost*." (Lk 19:2-10. Italic emphasis added by author.)

Zacchaeus was a chief tax collector, the supervisor of tax collectors. In occupied Israel, tax collectors were considered to be collaborators with the Roman enemy and thieves. For many years, Zacchaeus probably stole from anyone from whom it was possible to steal. Most likely, his conscience was burdened by numerous grave sins. The One who came *to seek and to save those who were lost* never stopped knocking on his door and, one day, this tax collector, Zacchaeus, heard the knocking.

When Zacchaeus realized that Jesus had arrived to his city of Jericho, he began to behave like an evangelical child. He climbed up a tree, paying no attention to the comical appearance of his situation, and waited, perhaps subconsciously, for God to pass. Although Zacchaeus was a very wealthy man, most likely the citizens of Jericho did not respect him. Finally, though, the citizens of Jericho had their chance to ridicule Zacchaeus, the person who had repeatedly stolen from them. They undoubtedly pointed their fingers at him and derided Zacchaeus as he sat in the tree. Zacchaeus, on the other hand, paid no attention to anyone. Instead, he agreed to be ridiculed by the people of Jericho as though human opinion no longer mattered to him. The only important person to Zacchaeus was Jesus, the One for whom he waited.

Some people in the crowd probably thought that Jesus would know all about who Zacchaeus really was, and that He would not even look at him. Why would the prophet from Nazareth pay any attention to such a sinner? Meanwhile, as He was passing by, Christ not only noticed Zacchaeus, but He also began a dialogue with him and pronounced some surprising words: "Zacchaeus, come down quickly, for today I must stay at your house." What prompted Jesus to decide that He **had** to visit the home of such a sinner?

There must have been something of the attitude of someone poor in spirit – someone full of folly – in Zacchaeus' behavior. The tax collector, Zacchaeus, was a true prodigal son in whom a new richness was born – a richness of humility and trust that allowed him to await everything from Jesus. When Zacchaeus discovered God's love, he simply became crazy with joy. Zacchaeus was completely different from the rich young man because he was ready to give away his fortune, even though Jesus did not demand this of him at all.

Throughout his entire life, Zacchaeus tediously stashed away the money that he had stolen from others every time the occasion arose. He strove to multiply his riches. However, after meeting Jesus, he wanted to cause his own financial ruin by giving away everything that he had acquired. He did not simply fulfill the requirements of the law, which required that, to make up for one's own faults, a thief would be required to give away one fifth more than he had stolen: "The LORD said to Moses, 'Tell the Israelites: If a man (or woman) commits a fault against his fellow man and wrongs him, thus breaking faith with the LORD, he shall confess the wrong he has done, restore his ill-gotten goods in full, and in addition give one fifth of their value to the one he has wronged'" (Num 5:5-7). Zacchaeus, however, promised to return four times as much as he owed to everyone whom he had cheated. In addition, he even promised to give half of his possessions away to the poor. If there were many people of whom Zacchaeus had taken advantage, then instead of remaining wealthy, he could have very easily become as poor as a beggar. Yet, because of his encounter with God's love, everything else became insignificant. The only thing that mattered to him was that he had met God and that he was conquered by the folly of faith. We can assume that the situation in which Zacchaeus found himself helped him to more deeply discover the truth about his spiritual misery. He became more convinced of how greedy and merciless he was and he lost all illusions about himself. Therefore, he could not count on any of his own merits as he went out to meet Jesus.

Zacchaeus, like the prodigal son, was able, only in the attitude of spiritual poverty, to count on the Father's goodness and to be open to His mercy. Thus, when it turned out that he, a sinner, would host in his home Someone who showed him true love – who in essence is pure love – a great desire to respond to this love was born in him. He understood that reparation for his evil alone would be an insufficient response. Thus, he wanted to lose possibly everything in order to become poor. Out of love for God he renounced everything to which he had dedicated his life – everything that, prior to his meeting with Christ, he loved and valued. Thanks to the attitude of spiritual poverty, Zacchaeus was able to receive true riches from God, who is the highest good. Jesus' words also attest to this: "Today salvation has come to this house . . ." (Lk 19:9).

After Jesus met with the rich young man, He said to His disciples: "Amen, I say to you it will be hard for one who is rich to enter the kingdom of heaven. Again I say to you, it is easier for a camel to pass through the eye of a needle than for the one who is rich to enter the kingdom of heaven" (Mt 19:23-24) Christ warns us against placing our trust in material or spiritual riches. Both Zacchaeus and the rich young man were rich in material possessions. Zacchaeus, though, was able to give up his possessions for Christ because, after he saw his spiritual misery, he trusted God and became poor in spirit. The rich young man was too "perfect" to take that step.

A person who is poor in spirit is free from attachment to anything because he knows that nothing really belongs to him. Upon discovering God's love, he desires to be in the arms of Christ as if he were an object that has no rights or freedom, like a balloon that is being carried by the wind of the Holy Spirit. Someone who is poor in spirit is like an evangelical child who desires to be obedient in everything and never says "no" to God, even in a difficult experience that he does not understand.

You, also, should not try too hard to understand everything that happens to you. Instead, try to trust God. After all, you are His son or daughter and you have nothing to fear. Can anyone deprive you of your birthright? Or, can anyone take away your right to Redemption? You can only despise Everything and, like the rich young man, sadly depart from God, who loves you.

Do not be surprised when you discover more and more of your misery and nothingness on your path to God.

If this did not occur, then you would be like the rich young man. Therefore, thank God for each truth that He reveals to you. Desire to be God's servant. Long to be someone who is poor in spirit and trusts his Lord so much that he does not ask unnecessary questions.

If something of the poor in spirit's folly arises within you, then you will "mirror" Mary's attitude that leads to full union with Christ.

SENSITIVITY TO THE SUBTLEST PROMPTINGS OF GOD

Not everyone who faces life's great storms and becomes submissive to God's will always remains faithful to God like Zacchaeus. A brick that is carried off by a hurricane does not necessarily change forever into a balloon that is sensitive to every gust of wind. If you do not take advantage of the graces that special storms in your life bring, then your life will barely change after the storm passes.

If you see, in the light of God's grace, that you resemble a brick rather than a balloon, then do not wait for a hurricane to hit you and your surroundings. Rather, acknowledge the truth that you are very attached to your own plans. Admit that you are closed to God's call. Confess that, in relation to the promptings of the Holy Spirit, you are as dead and heavy as a brick. From the depth of your misery, call upon the Blessed Mother:

> Mary, carry me in your arms like your own child. Please allow me to become light like a balloon carried by the wind of the Holy Spirit, docile to carrying out God's will and free from attachments. I do not want to know where this Divine Wind comes from or to where it will carry me. I do not want to impose my own plans and visions on God. I want to be docile like you.

Once you pray in this way, Mary will lift you up into her arms and, even if you still remain heavy and resistant like a brick, she will carry you where the Holy Spirit wants to lead you. She is the one who is fully sensitive to the subtlest promptings of the Spirit. She is the one who is always obedient to Him.

THE HUNGER FOR GOD'S WILL

You constantly meet God in your daily life. He is present to you through everything that He creates. You encounter God in people and events. In a special way, you also come across Him through His will. Through His will, God comes to you as if in His Own Person. God's will is not only something, it is also Somebody. God Himself comes to you with a concrete call. God reveals to you all that is salvific and, simultaneously, the best for you.[32]

---

[32] The word "salvific" means "tending to save, causing salvation." *Oxford English Dictionary*, s.v. "Salvific."

In answer to His call, what attitude does the Lord expect from us? This becomes clear when we take a look at what kind of attitude Jesus assumed when fulfilling the Father's will. Jesus said, ". . . I do not seek my own will but the will of the one who sent me," and "My food is to do the will of the one who sent me and to finish his work" (Jn 5:30, 4:34). Why did Jesus compare fulfilling God's will to food? This comparison shows us that our Lord could not live without fulfilling the will of the Father. Jesus sought God's will with determination, just like a starving person seeks food. Fulfilling God's will constantly nourished Him. At the same time, He was always hungry for it. He lived consumed by this hunger and was never satisfied, even though His hunger was constantly satisfied. The hunger to fulfill God's will lies at the base of each of the words and deeds of the One who became "obedient to death, / even death on a cross" (Phil 2:8).

Christ's extraordinary hunger to do God's will is the ideal example and role model for us to imitate. The person who hungers to fulfill God's will is the one who widely opens the door to the One who is knocking. The more you **empty yourself of your own will** and become poor in spirit, the wider you will open the door. As a result, you will be free for the coming of the Lord and His will, which is love. He desires to heal you and fill you with Himself.

The poorer you are, the hungrier you will be for God's will. The word "hunger" is ideal to use here. Hunger does not place conditions: the hungrier you are, the less picky you are about the food you eat. Sometimes it is enough to hunger for only half a day in order to eat everything that you are given, without being picky at all about what kind of food it is, even if you do not like it.

If a true hunger for God's will existed in us, then we would receive His will with joy and longing. More precisely, the plans and designs of each one of us would be secondary. In this way, would we not avoid many painful moments that come when we are so anxiously preoccupied with clinging to our own plans, even though God clearly calls these plans into question? In other words, the less we are attached to our own designs and conceptions, the more we become free to fulfill God's will. Consequently, it is easier for us to renounce everything that is not in accordance with His will.

The poverty of a person's own desires opens his heart to fulfilling God's desires. Such an attitude is salvific. It frees us from excessive self-preoccupation and fear about the future. If we truly believe that God desires that we assume precisely this attitude, then is there anything to fear? Can our merciful Father desire anything other than what is good for His beloved children?

It is necessary for you to hunger for everything that God wants to give to you, regardless of whether it is joy, suffering or even death. Even if God wants to give you success or difficulties, praise or unjust accusations, human friendship or loneliness and misunderstanding, you should hunger for it, because, if these gains and losses in life are according to His will, then they are salvific.

If a hunger for God's will arises within you, then you will discover, with much surprise, that it no longer matters to you what it will be. Is anything else as important? There is only one essential question: What could be more important than God's will, especially if God, who loves you and gave His life for your salvation, desires and planned precisely this for you?

What happens if someone lacks the hunger for God's will? Well, if we stop experiencing physical hunger for many days, then we forget that we have to eat. We could become seriously ill or even die as a result of malnutrition. Likewise, if a person has no spiritual hunger and is not nourished by God's will, then his soul, deprived of food, is as good as dead. Even though such a person might have been greatly successful and obtained everything that the world has to offer, he is dead. Only those who are unceasingly fed by fulfilling the will of God live because they feel the hunger for God's will.

When you desire and await the will of God, as you might desire and long for a glass of water in the desert, then everything else will be less significant. You will cease being attached to the riches of your own plans and designs. You will become poor and, therefore, freer than ever. This kind of poverty opens the borders of your own will's egoistic kingdom widely to God, the One who comes to you in order to reveal His promptings and plans. God desires to express His infinite love in this way.

Perhaps, when you hear God calling, you do not realize how much He wants to bestow upon you. By proposing to you His own will, He desires to free you from all of your wounds, disappointments, and difficulties, which are the result of seeking your own will. When you agree to let go of the steering wheel of your life and hand it over to a Father who loves you, then you will be freed from many fears and stress, as well as from **the torment of responsibility, which flows from the faith you have in yourself.** God does not want you to be so tormented. He desires to lift this weight from your shoulders and replace it with the **sweet burden of His will.** You only have to surrender to Him, and He will lead you.

If you attempt to seek Jesus, you will enter into an amazing communion with the Lord, and you will begin to look at everything as if through His eyes. This is a completely **new way of seeing the world.** A person, in whom the hunger to fulfill God's will is born, distances himself from all other values. Compared to the will of God, everything that he could possibly possess during his entire life becomes, in reality, insignificant. The only thing that really matters to him is to live with the hunger to do God's will.

Among all people, Mary most fully lived with a hunger for God's will. She was constantly hungry for God's will. This was her singular desire, the only program of her life. She longs to teach this attitude to every one of her children. She desires that you, too, hunger for God's will as she hungers for it. Moreover, Mary's *fiat*, uttered during the

Annunciation, testifies to her desire to fulfill God's will: "Behold, I am the handmaid of the Lord. May it be done to me according to your word" (Lk 1:38). Mary constantly longed for the Lord's Word, for His will. Is it not true that even today we can hear Mary's longing in her "May it be done to me," uttered ages ago? In this way, the Blessed Mother loved her beloved God before all else.

To love God means to love His will. The will of God is revealed to us in its splendor as the highest value for which to live. Jesus was able to fill Mary's soul in the most amazing way because her soul was free and empty for His love, and because Mary had ardently fallen in love with His will. The degree to which you love the will of the Father in heaven is the degree to which you, too, will be able to become brother, sister, and mother to Him. For, ". . . whoever does the will of [the] heavenly Father is [Jesus'] brother, and sister, and mother" (Mt 12:50).

POVERTY THAT OPENS TO FULLNESS

The merciful Samaritan cared for the wounded Israelite. This was possible only because this weak and wounded Israelite was ready to receive help, even from a stranger. Only someone who experiences the burden of sickness opens himself to the full care of the physician as the physician stoops down to him in order to help. The light of God, who knocks on the doors of our hearts, can be received only to the extent of our human insufficiency. We experience this insufficiency only to the extent to which we discover the truth about our own limitations and poverty. Only someone who has nothing stretches out his empty hand so that it may be filled with everything that is necessary to live.

Will a wealthy man await an endowment? Only in our poverty do we need help. And, only in poverty do we await the evangelical "everything," the coming of the Redeemer. If a person's poverty deepens, then this person will open himself to the fullness of the coming of God, so that the One who knocks no longer has to impose. The more you become poor in spirit, the more you will be open to Christ, who desires to give you everything. He is not satisfied with giving just any gift. He is waiting for your poverty to deepen to the extent that you will finally desire not only His gifts, but also Christ Himself and the fullness of His coming.

CHAPTER NINE

THE TRUTH ABOUT THAT WHICH PASSES AWAY

There are some very privileged moments in your life: when your plans fall apart, when you become sick, or when somebody to whom you are much attached and very close is no longer a part of your life. These moments, although difficult, are a privilege because they point out to you that God is knocking on the door of your heart. Through these events, He attempts to remind you about the truth that you are only on a journey on this earth and that everything that happens to you is subject to the law of passing away.[33]

---

[33] St. Paul, in his first letter to the Corinthians states, "I tell you, brothers, the time is running out. From now on, let those having wives act as not having them, those weeping as not weeping, those rejoicing as not rejoicing, those buying as not owning, those using the world as not using it fully. For the world in its present form is passing away" (7:29-31). From this passage, Paul indicates that everything that is of this world — people, objects, life, the world itself, etc. — inevitably passes away, meaning that everything is subject to time and death. Only God who is eternal does not pass away: "Yet the world and its enticement are passing away. But whoever does the will of God remains forever" (1 Jn 2:17). Therefore, everything that is subject to time and death may be understood as being subject to the "law of passing away."

Thomas À. Kempis, the author of *The Imitation of Christ*, describes the individual as a pilgrim, a wanderer who should maintain a distance from all temporal things by putting his trust in Christ:

> This world is not your permanent home; wherever you may be, you are a stranger, a pilgrim passing through. You will never find peace unless you are united with Christ in the very depths of your heart.
>
> Why do you look around here to find peace when you do not really belong here? Your place is in heaven, and you should see everything else in terms of heaven. All things pass away, and you pass away with them too. See that you do not cling to passing things, lest you become caught up in them and perish along with them.
>
> Let your highest thoughts be with the Most High and your prayer be directed to Christ without ceasing. (Thomas À Kempis, *The Imitation of Christ, Thomas À Kempis: A Timeless Classic for Contemporary Readers*, trans. William C. Creasy [Notre Dame, IN: Ave Maria Press, 1998], bk.2, chap.1, p. 65.)

This path on which we travel to fullness entails faithfulness to Christ's call to separate ourselves from our illusory attachments. The call also entails that we must not place our hearts in anything which we pass on the path – anything that will not reconcile us with the pilgrimage to our true homeland. When traveling toward this fullness, we must gradually rise to the freedom of spiritual poverty of a soul that does not want to be rooted in this world. While traveling along this path, we have to lose everything of which we are possessive and everything that we attributed to ourselves. In turn, by becoming poor and, through this poverty, free, we can travel farther along the path that leads to union with the Lord.

"YOU ARE DUST, AND TO DUST YOU WILL RETURN"

After the fall, our first parents heard very strong words, "For you are dirt, / and to dirt you shall return" (Gen 3:19). In this way, God formulated the law of passing away and the law of temporality to which every person on the earth is subject. Only a human soul is immortal. All other material things are subject to time – they, including our earthly life, are passing away.

We cannot stop time. Here on earth we are travelers, who have to unceasingly journey on the pilgrimage to our heavenly homeland. The world in which we live and everything upon which a person, thanks to God's grace, builds, are subject to the law of passing away. Someone who is poor in spirit **knows and accepts** this truth about the temporal order of the things of this world. Can we possess the water that passes through our fingers? Is it worthwhile to be preoccupied with making the effort to possess a flowing stream? Our countless attachments bind our hearts to things of this world, which do not last and things that will disappear like a flowing stream of water. All of our worries, preoccupations, bitterness, and disappointments come from our possessiveness and our attempts to rule over that which we cannot rule.

Certainly, our attitude toward the world should be respectful because the world is created by God. He sustains its existence and is constantly present in it. The things that surround us are like the landscape at which we glance as we pass along the path. These things were created to last only a certain amount of time; they were created so that we can use them to fulfill God's will and thus unite our wills with His holy will. The things of this world are meant to serve our sanctification. Therefore, it is important that we treat things of this world in an instrumental way by maintaining a proper distance from them – the distance of spiritual poverty.

We have to take advantage of everything in a **worthy** way, **according to** God's will. Everything that God gives us is only a means to serve the end of becoming more deeply united with Him. The fragility and lack of stability of everything in the world should remind us that, apart from God, everything is nothing. Our relationship to everything should be that of a traveler as he makes his way toward God. Our bodies are also fragile and subject to the law of passing away. In a practical way, aging convinces us of this; as we grow older, we lose our strength and physical fitness. Even when we take the greatest care of our health, which is the right thing to do, we cannot stop the slow process of dying. This process is not easy to accept. When we see that our bodies are similar to everything else by which we pass on the path, it provides a great opportunity for us to grow in the attitude of spiritual poverty and the sense of being totally dependent on God. Thanks to our physical weaknesses, we can experience more fully the meaning of the words, "Without me you can do nothing" (Jn 15:5). As a consequence, we will be able to cling more strongly to God.

BUILDING CASTLES OUT OF SNOW

When you believe in your own strength, you live as if God does not exist. Also, you behave as if the law of passing away does not exist, as if you will live on earth forever. A person who does not accept his status as a pilgrim and ignores the law of passing away is similar to someone who builds a large castle out of snow and does not realize that, when spring arrives, his great snow castle will melt to a mere puddle. Even if someone considers himself wealthy because he owns a beautiful castle, he is really only a pitiful beggar. Only the attitude of spiritual poverty gives us freedom from illusions because in due time, all illusions have to melt away in God's light of truth.

When we remember about our status as pilgrims, it helps us to maintain a certain distance of spiritual poverty from the world. It shields us from excessive involvement in things and relationships that are essentially short-lived. On the path to fulfillment, thanks to the attitude of spiritual poverty, we engage in various activities only to the extent to which it is God's will, rather than giving our hearts to those things.

We do not know the plans that God has for us. Therefore, it is necessary to maintain the proper distance from everything of "value." For example, when learning a new language, it is easy to give into the illusion that you are acquiring something of lasting and unchanging value. Yet, this is not true. A single injury, even a slight damage to the brain, is sufficient to completely wipe out your memory, just like a magnetic tape that has been erased. Due to this brain injury, you could have serious difficulties communicating even in your native language, let alone the foreign language that you had previously learned with such difficulty.

It is unwise if we look at everything that we have acquired in our lives without the consciousness that everything *is dust, and to dust it will return.* Constantly thinking about the law of passing away, without being open to God, can result in discouragement, apathy, or even severe depression. In the end, is it worthwhile to be so preoccupied with everything that we acquire, since these things are only dust, ashes, which we will have to leave behind in order to advance along our pilgrimage?

God wants us to obtain this dust in order to fulfill His will. Because God expects this from us, we have to participate in certain activities. We are not supposed to do this to feed our egoism and pride. Instead, we do this only because of Him. Moreover, God wants us to continue building castles from snow. He does not want us to place our hope in them, however. We must remember that one day all of our castles will melt away without a trace. If everything that we do does not pertain to eternal things, then everything will pass away.

Our days are numbered. We do not know how many more days we have left to live. Consequently, it is better to live one day at a time. We must approach everything with great involvement and with the love that God expects from us. At the same time, we must do everything as if tomorrow we will have to move on and leave it all behind. Our hearts are created for God and only for Him. It is not worthwhile to surrender our hearts to the things and matters that you pass by as you walk along the path. A person who is poor in spirit always remembers that everything he does is only a means to union with the Lord. Everything is but a step on the path that leads to fulfillment.

When the time comes for you to lose things, you will become convinced that some things in your life are lasting, while other things are no more than mere castles built of snow. In the rays of God's grace, your empire of snow – your positive self-image, knowledge, capabilities, relationships, reliance on your surroundings, social status, health, and physical fitness – will begin to melt. Even your spiritual castles – your zeal in service to God, your piety, and your ease at prayer – will pass away. If you suffer when your illusory riches turn into puddles, then this is a sign that you still lack the attitude of a person who is poor in spirit. This indicates that you are attached to things that pass away like snow. Sometimes such snow castles begin to melt even as you build them. It is even possible that you will not be able to finish building your snow castle because the snow will melt before you see any results of your work. For example, perhaps you are learning a new language because it is God's will. However, despite your many efforts, you experience a lack of progress. You still make many mistakes, forget words, and fail to comprehend much. Despite this, you do not give up. You continue to work. You say to God:

> Lord, if you want everything that I do to melt in my hands, then I also desire this.

If it is God's will that you build something out of snow, it is not worth it to consider whether you are doing something that will last or not. For the person who is poor in spirit, the only thing that matters is that he builds for Christ and His glory. Mary teaches us such an attitude. She was able to see God in every created thing. At the same time, she remained detached from these things. She knew that everything that surrounded her was only dust and to dust it would return. The law of passing away was very deeply impressed upon her heart.

Mary is our role model of the attitude of spiritual poverty. She participated in everything just as God desired because she knew that any other attitude would be an unacceptable offense to God because it would be like living as if He does not exist. If you have formed excessive attachments to anything in place of God, then you offend God and bring suffering upon yourself. Your Mother, however, wants to protect you from such attachments. Mary is always with you. Therefore, you can ask her to be detached for you and on your behalf from everything that you do so that you can maintain **freedom of heart**. If you are open like a child to the graces that God wants to give you through Mary, then you can and will be prevented from forming excessive attachments.

At work, in studies, in endeavors undertaken for the church, as well as in all other things, there is only one thing that matters. **Only God and you** matter – you whom God chooses and directs toward complete union with Him. Our Lord desires that, upon being united with Him, you live a deeper life of faith. He wants you to be poor in spirit by refusing to rely on the goods that you pass on the path, and by relying instead only on those things that are eternal – His power and His love.

CHAPTER TEN

DYING TO ONE'S SELF AS FREEDOM FROM ILLUSIONS

When cleansing us from illusions, Our Lord God does not take any real goods away from us. Instead, He opens us to the truth. If He takes something away from us, then He does so because it is merely fictional or it is a falsehood behind which there is only emptiness. For example, behind a beautiful theater curtain, the set is really make-believe, even if the actors appear on stage and act out real events.

The breakdown of our fantasies, falsehoods, and illusory supports leads us to an ongoing process of dying to one's self. This process is tedious and difficult because, within themselves, illusions contain the poison of pleasure. Each of our illusions is pleasurable. Otherwise, it would not lure us in and give rise to the greed of reliance in us. We are afraid to die to ourselves because it seems to us that we are losing something that is of real value. Meanwhile, what really matters in this process is that we shed our delusions that something really exists in the emptiness behind the beautiful theater curtain.

Attachment to pleasure, generated by our illusory supports, is so strong that God reveals this attachment to us very slowly and gradually so as not to wound us too much. He expects us to accept this process of dying. God wants us to consent to the burning away of all delusions that seduce us by their deceptive sense of goodness. Although imperceptible to the human eye, God can carve a masterpiece from a person who resembles a piece of wood. God desires to create in us His Own image and the fullness of His presence. St. John of the Cross describes this process through a metaphor of a piece of wood immersed in a flame.[34] Just as a piece of wood is immersed in a flame, so too does human misery become like ash transformed by and united with the resplendent power of the flame of God's

---

[34] St. John of the Cross uses a piece of wood immersed in the Divine Flame as metaphor for purification and transformation of the soul in Divine Love: "For the sake of further clarity in this matter, we ought to note that this purgative and loving knowledge, or divine light we are speaking of, has the same effect on a soul that fire has on a log of wood. The soul is purged and prepared for union with the divine light just as the wood is prepared for transformation into the fire. Fire, when applied to wood, first dehumidifies it, dispelling all moisture and making it give off any water it contains. Then it gradually turns the wood black, makes it dark and ugly, and even causes it to emit a bad odor. By drying out the wood, the fire brings to light and expels all those ugly and dark accidents that are contrary to fire. Finally, by heating and enkindling it from without, the fire transforms the wood into itself and makes it as beautiful as it is itself. Once transformed, the wood no longer has any activity or passivity of its own, except for its weight and its quantity that is denser than the fire. It possesses the properties and performs the actions of the fire: It is dry and it dries; it is hot and it gives off heat; it is brilliant and it illumines; it is also much lighter in weight than before. It is the fire that produces all these properties in the wood." John of the Cross, *The Dark Night*, 2.10.1.

love. So too can any ordinary, or even ugly, piece of wood be sculpted and transformed into a masterpiece.

It is an extraordinary grace to discover that human supports are illusory. These illusions are like congealed forms of ash that fall apart upon their first contact with the Divine Flame. This special action of God's light shows us what a tragedy it would be if we continued to rely on our worthless illusions. Our experiences with the fragility of human supports push us into the arms of God, toward the altar, toward fullness as described in the vision of St. Faustina Kowalska.[35]

IF THE GRAIN DOES NOT DIE

Referring to His approaching suffering and death, Jesus spoke about the death of a grain of wheat, "Amen, amen, I

---

[35] The following is an excerpt from St. Maria Faustina Kowalska's Diary, describing this vision: "Once I saw a big crowd of people in our chapel, in front of the chapel and in the street, because there was no room for them inside. The chapel was decorated for a feast. There were a lot of clergy near the altar, and then our sisters and those of many other congregations. They were all waiting for the person who was to take a place on the altar. Suddenly I heard a voice saying that I was to take the place on the altar. But as soon as I left the corridor to go across the yard and enter the chapel, following the voice that was calling me, all the people began to throw at me whatever they had to hand: mud, stones, sand, brooms, to such an extent that I at first hesitated to go forward. But the voice kept on calling me even more earnestly, so I walked on bravely. When I entered the chapel, the superiors, the sisters, the students, and even my parents started to hit me with whatever they could, and so whether I wanted to or not, I quickly took my place on the altar. As soon as I was there, the very same people, the students, the sisters, the superiors and my parents all began to hold their arms out to me asking for graces; and as for me, I did not bear any grudge against them for having thrown all sorts of things at me, and I was surprised that I felt a very special love precisely for those persons who had forced me to go more quickly to my appointed place. At the same time my soul was filled with ineffable happiness, and I heard these words, **Do whatever you wish, distribute graces as you will, to whom you will and when you will.** Then, instantly, the vision disappeared." Maria Faustina Kowalska, Diary, Divine Mercy in My Soul, (Stockbridge, MA: Marians of the Immaculate Conception, 2003), Diary 31.

say to you, unless a grain of wheat falls to the ground and dies, it remains just a grain of wheat; but if it dies, it produces much fruit" (Jn 12:24). These words of Christ also pertain to each of us. If we resist dying to ourselves, then our lives will remain fruitless. We will not take advantage of the designs and hopes that God has with regard to each one of us. It is not possible to deepen our bond with God without dying to ourselves, namely, without dying to our pride and our egoism. The process of becoming poor in spirit entails reevaluating our relationship to temporal things and people. Moreover, how this happens depends on the will of God for each one of us.

Certainly, dying to one's self is a necessary process, and God awaits our consent to it. The grain dies so that the kingdom of God, the kingdom that can expand only at the cost of the death of our illusions, will grow. In one of the parables Christ said: "It is like a mustard seed that, when it is sown in the ground, is the smallest of all the seeds on the earth. But, once it is sown, it springs up and becomes the largest of plants and puts forth large branches, so that the birds of the sky can dwell in its shade" (Mk 4:31-32). To cultivate a large shrub from a small seed, the seed must be sown in the winter so that it can die. The condition of the soil must be just right so that the seed will first die, and then the process of germination will occur.

Where is our soil, our place to die? It is the environment in which we live. In a way, it is our decision because we choose in which kind of environment we will live.

We choose with whom we will have close relationships. Thus, to a certain extent, we choose the soil in which we, as seeds, will die to ourselves and bring forth the expected fruits from God.

WHEN THE GRAIN BEGINS TO BREAK

When the grain that is sown in the soil begins to open as the first sprout of new life breaks through, its situation seems to be very dramatic and even terrifying. For, even if we know quite well that this process signifies the loss of our illusory and false riches, normally this knowledge is purely theoretical. Moreover, the grain of our spiritual life can be quite terrified because of what is happening to it, even if it knows that the process of dying leads to new life.

Very often we behave as if we are trying to protect this grain of our spiritual life and prevent it from breaking by wrapping it up. We do everything possible to hold it together. Some people are even willing to change their environment. They are willing to choose a new and even infertile place so that they remain a grain. In various ways we try to counteract this process because it is the beginning of dying to ourselves and the end of that which was. As we focus all of our attention on our painful experiences, we forget that really only a world of soap bubbles is dying in us and not the real value for which life is worth living.

The drama of the bursting of the grain arises from our lack of sufficient faith – the faith that allows us to accept everything that God intends for us, even if God's will, which desires to liberate us from various kinds of illusions, remains unclear or we do not understand it.

THE FREEING OUTLOOK OF FAITH

If you attempt to look at the process of dying to yourself with faith, then everything that you so painfully experience will push you toward God. You will see that everything that you lose in this process – wealth, honor, and status – passes away, or vanishes like rotting garbage.

Is it worthwhile to cry about something that enslaves? Is it worthwhile to cry about that which captivates us, but, when seen in the light of faith, is only garbage and ceases to be the object of our desires and longings? We should only find support for our feet in the goods of this world. In other words, we should consider the goods of this world as footholds on which we may step and even trample along our path to God. We do not adore the ground on which we walk. We treat it only as a firm foundation on which we may walk along the way to our goal.

Why is your heart so afraid, so troubled? Our loving Father detaches you as delicately as possible from all that enslaves you and stops you on the path to Him. You still cry instead of thanking Him. St. John of the Cross says: "It makes little difference whether a bird is tied by a thin thread or by a cord. Even if it is tied by thread, the bird will be held bound just as surely as if it were tied by cord; that is, it will be impeded from flying as long as it does not break the thread. Admittedly, the thread is easier to break, but no matter how easily this may be done, the bird will not fly away without first doing so."[36] The bird restrained by a cord cannot free itself. Likewise, we are incapable of freeing ourselves from illusions that attract and enslave us. If God destroys our illusions by severing us from all of their entangling threads, should we not be grateful to Him for this great grace?

Do not focus on that which is painful for you in the process of dying. Try to see Christ in every situation with the eyes of faith. For, He frees you from wayward illusions and forms of imprisonment that lead you away from Him and make it impossible for you to draw closer to Him. Disappointments occur only for those who do not look at their losses through the eyes of faith. They bring about bitterness and suffering, which are actually only the bursting of the soap bubbles of our illusions. Does it make sense to cry when you lose them? If you live only for those soap bubbles, how can you be a pilgrim? How can you strive for and move toward the real goal rather than the illusionary one? Acknowledging that dying to yourself is the optimal program of your life will be the result of the efforts of your mind and will. Your emotions and your feelings, however, will defy these efforts. Therefore, you should often repeat to yourself:

> I want to believe that everything that happens to me leads me to new life, even though it is so difficult and painful.

---

[36] John of the Cross, *Ascent of Mount Carmel*, 1.11.4.

171

The **less you concentrate on yourself,** the more resistance to your wounded self you will develop. Normally your resistance is as weak as your faith is weak. Saints accepted this process of dying to themselves much like the shedding of dried skin, because their hearts were not attached to anything except for God. Your dying, however, should be subjected to certain controls. Even a grain dies most efficiently under the watchful eye of the gardener. He properly prepares and fertilizes the soil, tills and waters it, and then observes the growth of the grain. The confessor and/or spiritual guide can be the gardener of your soul and a special instrument in the hands of God. If you desire to cooperate with him, then Christ will be able to take care of you through this instrument in order to ensure that your illusions will die and a *new person* will grow within you according to God's will.

Unlike a grain, a person has free will. After being sown, a grain automatically begins to grow. It is subject only to the conditions of the environment in which it is found. A human being, on the other hand, is free and has to decide on his own whether or not he will agree or disagree to be subjected to any such process. Everything depends on the free decision of the individual. A new sprout feeds off of the substance of the grain. Similarly, new life grows in you at the cost of the life of the old person, who has to undergo annihilation. Obviously, not everything that constitutes your old life will have to die. When you pull out a shaft of wheat from the soil, you can find the husk amongst the roots, a remnant of the grain from which it sprang forth. When new life is born in us, the husk that is the old person, a remnant of our illusions, nourished in the past, will remain.

Complete transformation will take place only at the moment of death. This will be the last stage of the pilgrimage for those who achieve union with God while here on this earth and die as saints. At the moment of death, a saint dies to himself completely, and Christ leads him across the threshold to the fullness of new life in a new, glorified and divinized body. This is the final goal of our earthly pilgrimage. During this pilgrimage, we have to agree that the old person in us has to die. Do not be afraid, therefore, of the changes that take place in the relations that rule your life. **Do not be afraid of dying to yourself.** Also, do not be afraid when the process of dying will gradually encompass all aspects of your life that were endangered by the charm of will o' the wisps.[37]

When we look at the life of the Blessed Mother, we can see that she is submissive to the will and action of God in everything. This openness to God's will always protected her from various kinds of waywardness. The one who always said "yes" to the Lord, the one who called herself the handmaid of the Lord, always fulfilled the will of God perfectly much like a grain that surrenders itself to different processes in accordance with the designs of the Creator. Likewise, this must be the same with you and your stance

---

[37] Will o' the wisp is an erroneous perception of reality.

toward everything that God intends for you. Try to be submissive and totally obedient to God's light that knocks in order to allow you to be purified from layers of various decaying illusions and mirages. This will allow you to surrender to His promptings according to Mary's example. St. John of the Cross employed the image of wood burned up in the flames of God's love in order to describe the process of our union with God.[38] This process of being burned up results in the death of all of our illusions regarding who we are. During this process, we must stand in truth about our spiritual misery before God, so that the grace of God completely penetrates our souls. When this happens, we will become instruments that God will be able to use for the realization of His plans, not only for our dear ones, but also for those whom we will never even know. We will become instruments that will change the world.

---

[38] John of the Cross, *The Dark Night*, 2.10.1.

CHAPTER ELEVEN

THE GREATEST BESTOWAL

C an one force another to love, when that other loves something else and has turned his heart in another direction? The love of God needs our poverty of solitude. God's love needs solitude of spirit, which is another definition of spiritual poverty. This solitude is freedom of heart from inappropriate concerns, efforts, and excessive worry about oneself and others. It is freedom from the hustle and bustle of this world, and it allows us to continually hear the Lord when He calls us. Solitude is openness to the highest bestowing from God or, the Kingship of His will in us.

We should choose solitude as an empty place, or the space in which we encounter God, where nothing disturbs the soul's contemplation of the One who loves it. Only in solitude can a person be one on one with God. Therefore, that is why God fights for our solitude with Him. God does not want to force us, however. Instead, He patiently and humbly knocks so that we ourselves will want to choose this solitude with Him. He knocks so patiently that it seems endless because our wandering off toward the business of this world also seems endless.

Jesus' humble knocking during His long conversation with the Samaritan woman was fruitful because, due to her woundedness, she was an outcast. Because of this situation in her life, she was opened fully to the Savior who desired to rescue her. In this sense, in the final account, with His humble knocking God conquers our hearts that constantly flee from solitude and find themselves restless and lost amid the idols that the spirit of this world offers us.

GOD IS HIDDEN IN LONELINESS

To follow God, means that one must sooner or later choose poverty as loneliness for the Lord. If Christ said about Himself, "Foxes have dens and birds of the sky have nests, but the Son of Man has nowhere to rest his head" (Lk 9:58), then each person who chooses God and His will, just like the Master, is going to be poor like Christ in the sense that he will be homeless and deprived of shelter, of a place where he can rest his head.

Every person who wants to open himself up to God has to accept loneliness at home with his family, in a relationship with a husband or wife, and in raising children. It is necessary to fall in love with poverty at work, during prayer, and even in contact with those to whom we are united by spiritual bonds. If it were not for blessed loneliness, faith would not deepen in us, and we would never desire God before all else. In the light of faith, we see that we are certainly never alone because the Father who loves us is always close to us. Yet, who has such faith to really live with this consciousness? When we rely on people, we do not seek to rely on God. Only when we become poor, when we cannot rely on anyone or anything, will we turn to the Lord and begin to seek our support in Him. Cardinal Ratzinger states:

> Loneliness is indubitably one of the basic roots from which man's encounter with God grew up. Where man experiences his solitariness, he experiences at the same time how much his whole existence is a cry for the "You" and how ill-adapted he is to be only an "I" in himself. This loneliness can become apparent to a man on various levels. To start with it can be comforted by the discovery of a human "You". But then there is a paradox that, as Claudel says, [P. Claudel, *Le Soulier de Satin*—the great concluding dialogue between Dona Prouchèze and Rodrique] every "You" found by man finally turns out to be an unfulfilled and unfulfillable promise; that every "You" is at bottom another disappointment and that there comes a point when no encounter can surmount the final loneliness: the very process of finding and of having found thus becomes a pointer back to the loneliness, a call to the absolute "You" that really descends into the depths of one's own "I". (Joseph Cardinal Ratzinger, *Introduction to Christianity*, trans. J.R. Foster [San Francisco: Ignatius Press, 1990], 69-70.)

The grace of loneliness is one of the most precious gifts that God gives to us on our path to sanctity. We encounter the Lord in the deepest way, and our communion takes place with Him, in loneliness. Blessed is the poverty of loneliness in which a person discovers the truth about himself, as well as the truth about God and His love. By choosing loneliness, we choose truth; we choose God, who is hidden in loneliness. This kind of poverty does not have to be actual physical isolation or loneliness. After all, Christ spoke about His solitude when He was surrounded by friends – apostles – who loved Him and who were convinced that they were ready to die for Him. The grain of betrayal had not yet germinated even in the heart of Judas. But did the apostles entirely understand the meaning of the Lord's words?

Jesus' poverty was the loneliness of the One whose food was fulfillment of the Heavenly Father's will. If you want God and His will to become the only love of your life, then you will find the answer to how to imitate the Master, even when you are surrounded by a group of people who love you, precisely in loneliness.

Following Christ, and therefore embarking on the path to sanctity, leads through greater and greater denudation and solitude to Golgotha. Very often, from the very beginning, those who choose this path are misunderstood by friends, acquaintances, colleagues at work, family members and those closest to them. By failing to understand the special relationship that begins to unite us with God, those closest to us may not accept the path that we have chosen. As a result, the first discord with others because of Jesus happens in our lives. Moreover, in later stages of interior life, Jesus' statement may take place: "For I have come to set / a man 'against his father, / a daughter against her mother, / and a daughter-in-law against her mother-in-law; / and one's enemies will be those of his household'" (Mt 10:35-36). Experiencing the pain of being misunderstood is difficult. That is why Christ renews His Salvific Sacrifice for us each day by giving Himself to us in the Eucharist in order to bestow upon us His Own Divine power on this path.

Cardinal Ratzinger writes about the loneliness that our Lord Jesus Christ experienced in this way: "He gathered some friends, but the disappointment of a friendship that was betrayal was not spared him, nor the disappointment of being misunderstood by his apostles who were men of good will but weak. In the end he was to live alone on the Mount of Olives the hour of agony during which his disciples were asleep. He was misunderstood in his innermost nature."[39] Jesus was completely alone when He was apprehended because all of His disciples abandoned Him. Even before He was apprehended, He was completely alone as He prayed in the garden, for His disciples, despite His intense pleading, kept falling asleep. How lonely Jesus must have been when He stood before Pilate! How lonely He must have been when He was scourged! How lonely He must have been when He was scorned as He carried the Cross to Golgotha! In the face

---

[39] Joseph Cardinal Ratzinger, *The God of Jesus Christ*, trans. Robert J. Cunningham (Chicago: Franciscan Herald Press, 1979), 71-2.

of His Passion, Our Lord expressed His loneliness in the deepest way when He said, "*Eli, Eli, lema sabachthani?*" which means, "My God, my God, why have you forsaken me?" (Mt 27:46). These words reveal the infinite loneliness that our Savior must have felt in His human nature when He gave up His life for us. By following in His footsteps, we too should gradually lose all illusory supports and become poorer so that, at the end, there will remain the one and only true reliance – God and His love.

If you fall in love with and espouse poverty, then you will espouse God in it. Only a soul that sees that it is completely alone can fully receive God because it finds everything in Him and knows that, outside of Him, it has no one and nothing. Therefore, let us not be surprised by various denudations that we will experience on the path that leads to union with the Lord. These denudations help us to accept loneliness, which is the path toward union with God and the place where we encounter Him. However, if we do not consent to loneliness during our lifetime, then we will still encounter the Lord in total solitude at the moment of death. The sooner we begin loving the grace of loneliness as the place of our encounter with God, the better prepared we will be for our final encounter with Him at the moment of death.

When you run away from the poverty of loneliness, when you are afraid of it and continuously try to fill it with people or things, when you are alone and seek reliance on yourself, you essentially try to escape from God, from your Divine Spouse, with whom you can be united only in loneliness. Listen to how St. Teresa of Avila expresses her great conviction in loneliness: "*Solo Dios basta.*"[40] This means "God alone suffices." You, too, do not need anyone or anything other than Him.

Another kind of loneliness exists, and it is solitude chosen by the heart. Cardinal Ratzinger writes, "In addition to the solitude due to a lack of understanding, there was for Jesus another way of being alone. He lived his life by beginning from a center that others could not reach: his solitude with God."[41]

FREEDOM OF HEART

God does not want us to be attached to any of His gifts. We should possess them as if we do not posses them (cf. 1 Cor 7:29-31). After all, apart from God, nothing is ours. All of the goods that our merciful Father has entrusted to us are on loan. They are not our property. As faithful administrators, we should manage everything according to God's will and designs. This is why we cannot build our own plans and hopes on anything that we possess.

God wants us to accept the **distance of spiritual poverty** with regard to the people and things that surround us. Lack of acceptance of poverty and the process by which it deepens throughout the various stages of spiritual life are

---

[40] "Poesias 9" in *The Collected Works of St. Teresa of Avila*, trans. J. Cooney (Washington, DC: ICS Publications, 1987), 3:386.
[41] Ratzinger, *God of Jesus Christ*, 72.

very serious obstacles on the path to union with God. Poverty is freedom from attachments. When we run away from poverty, we fill the space of our lives with attachments. In doing so, we become, in a certain sense, like the things to which we are attached. However, if we are to be formed in the image and likeness of God, then we cannot be attached to anyone or anything apart from Him. When, by consenting to solitude, we receive God who is hidden in it, then we choose the path by which we will become formed more in His likeness – the path by which the divinization of our human natures will ultimately take place in heaven.

In *The Ascent of Mount Carmel*, St. John of the Cross very clearly states that anyone who is attached to creatures is in no way capable of union with the infinite being of God.[42] *Attachment to creatures* can be understood as reliance on people and things, as opposed to seeking reliance on the Creator of all things. St. John of the Cross defines this as *being captivated by the grace and elegance of creatures.* He asserts that the soul that chases after what is beautiful or pleasurable to it, cannot draw closer to the infinite beauty of God. Everything that, in our eyes, constitutes some value in and of itself is valueless in the eyes of our Lord. Even more, it is an obstacle to union with Him. Such things may be friendship, love, work, studies, or basically any value that is precious to us apart from God.[43] Thanks to the grace of poverty, we are forced to choose between God and the world of our own

---

[42] Cf. John of the Cross, *Ascent of Mount Carmel*, 1.4.4.
[43] Ibid.

illusions. When we attempt to run away from loneliness and to fill it with illusions, we start to treat objects as subjects. We even attribute divine characteristics to them. In doing this, we **divinize things** that are solely gifts from our Lord. We make idols out of creatures; we worship them instead of the true God.

For example, do not some people treat their new cars with such love and care that should really be shown more to people than to things? Similarly, we can be attached to a collection of very valuable coins that we have accumulated over many years, or to a collection of books or CDs that we have carefully selected. Even our fashionable clothing or elegant home furnishings can become objects of this kind of love. Love, as noted by St. John of the Cross, not only *creates a likeness between a lover and the object of love, it even brings the lover down to the level of the object of his love.*[44] If you love something created by God, but disregard God, then you surrender yourself to whatever you love and expel the Creator from your heart. In other words, you usher what you love, and that to which you unreservedly give yourself, into your soul, which is the temple of the Holy Spirit, and into the monstrance of your heart where Christ is hidden. What can you do to avoid expelling the Lord from your heart? What is necessary to prevent idols from taking the place of the Lord? How can you choose and love solitude? How can you receive God in the quietness of your heart and allow

---

[44] Ibid.

Him to form your soul as He desires? Before everything else, you have to lean on the truth about yourself – the truth about your misery. It is best to directly acknowledge the truth and humbly bring it to Jesus, saying:

> *Jesus, I am unable, and perhaps do not even want to choose You. That is why I run away from loneliness. I fill it with attachments. I worship people or things and turn them into idols. I throw You out from the temple of my soul, from the monstrance of my heart.*

If someone removes the Eucharist from the monstrance and adores something in place of it, as if this thing were the Body of Christ, then not only would he commit idolatry, but also horrifying sacrilege. When you discover how you treat God, even if you are not entirely aware of it, you will call out with determination:

> *Lord, have pity on me, a sinner. Give me Your grace because I am sold into slavery to sin. Even more, I do not want to be set free from sin at all. My only hope is Your mercy.*

Did the blind man from Jericho see any other option for himself other than to call out, "Jesus, son of David, have pity on me" (Mk 10:47)? Did the tax collector, who struck his breast as he prayed in the temple, pleading, "oh God, be merciful to me, / a sinner" (Lk 18:13) see any possibility for himself other than God's mercy? God never rejects the plea of a sinner who acknowledges that he has wasted everything and humbly begs Christ to rescue him. Christ came into the world precisely for such people; He came to save the lame and the sick. He came to rescue miserable sinners and those who see how desperately they need His mercy.

THOSE WHO GO BEFORE US ON THE PATH OF LONELINESS

Spiritual poverty is a characteristic of every saint; for, all saints were completely alone when they were united with God here on earth.

How poor St. Peter was when he denied his Master three times and then wept bitterly! Perhaps he saw how he had no reliance on anyone or anything, not even on himself. That is why, with contrition and in poverty, he turned to God as his only hope (cf. Lk 22:55-62).

The priest Zechariah was also alone as he served in the temple when the Lord revealed to him His plan related with the birth of John the Baptist. Zechariah was completely alone; he was unable to turn to anybody for advice or help. When he attempted to rely on his own mind and experience, the Lord made him mute. God wanted his servant to give up all of his supports by abandoning everything except God Himself. He desired that Zechariah fully accept His will (cf. Lk 1:5-25).

Abraham, the Father of Faith, was also alone when God directed him to offer his only son, Isaac, as a sacrifice. Abraham was unable to rely on his memory, his reason, or even his understanding of God's will. After all, Abraham was convinced that, upon offering such a sacrifice, he would nullify God's promise that his descendants would be as numerous as the stars in heaven. Nevertheless, this Patriarch, and saint, was ready to question his own understanding of God's ways. In complete poverty, he surrendered to the Lord, and he accepted His unfathomable will (cf. Gen 22:1-13).

No one, however, experienced so strongly the depths of poverty or understood it as well as Mary. Therefore, we can always ask her to accept loneliness in us. Otherwise, we will either always fearfully run away from this grace, or we will suffer a painful defeat by summoning up our own strength to make attempts to control loneliness. Mary experienced poverty throughout her entire life. During the Annunciation, she was alone and unable to rely on anyone or anything, not even on her own knowledge and reason. In poverty, the Mother of our Lord uttered her *fiat*. In solitude, she accepted the God-Man into her body and experienced the unfathomable mystery of the Incarnation (cf. Lk 1:26-38). She was also alone as she awaited the birth of her Son. For, St. Joseph learned nothing from Mary about the Annunciation. If God had not revealed this mystery to him, Mary would have never revealed to her husband what had happened to her (cf. Mt 1:18-25).

Mary was also alone during Jesus' childhood. While raising Him, she observed how the Savior of the world grew and developed. In solitude, she pondered the great works of God (cf. Lk 2:50-51). Later, she continued to live in a spirit of poverty as Jesus departed from home and began teaching in order to fulfill the Father's will. Her communion with her Son was permeated with spiritual poverty and with a complete lack of reliance on created things. For Mary, only faith remained.

Loneliness is given to us also so that we may learn how to find support in faith. Mary was completely alone at the foot of the Cross. Of all people, she participated in the most perfect way in the Passion of the Crucified One. Later, in solitude, she awaited His Resurrection. None of the apostles understood the mystery of Redemption like Mary; only she believed so strongly in Christ's words that she did not even run to His tomb in order to convince herself by seeing with her own eyes that it was empty.

The Blessed Mother was also alone as she waited with the apostles for the coming of the Holy Spirit. As Mary prayed, were the apostles able to understand how she – the temple of the Holy Spirit – awaited His descent upon the Church? After Pentecost, in silence and solitude, Mary accompanied the birth of the Church as its Mother. Because Mary is the Mother of the Church, it is so important for us to be open to her action in us. It is crucial that we hand ourselves over to her and to everything that God wants to accomplish in our souls through her. On our own, we will not accept the grace of loneliness. We will either fear it, or we will try to take control of it. Such a response only ends in defeat.

Loneliness is the place of encounter with God. At the same time, it is a difficult trial of faith. Therefore, we should never face it by relying on our own strength. Love for poverty, as solitude or loneliness because of love for the Lord, can only be built upon trust in God's mercy. Any attempt to choose solitude with our own strength is doomed to failure. If we try to imitate Jesus by relying on our own strength, then this will result in a great catastrophe, a psychological breakdown, or an escape and reliance on sin. We can love spiritual poverty only by uniting ourselves with God. Otherwise, it will always be a torment.

POVERTY AS PURITY OF HEART

Purity of heart means purity of intention, a supernatural relationship to the world. Poverty of heart entails looking at everything that surrounds us as God looks at it. A pure heart is permeated by God, submissive to His action, and cooperative with grace.

Impurity, on the other hand, arises in our hearts when we live as if God does not exist. Impurity of heart means that our will does not conform to God's will. When this happens, our relationships become impure to everything: the world surrounding us, the people, and the things that we encounter. The relationships are impure because we do not take God into account. Instead, we question His unique Lordship. If we looked at flowers in a pure way, then we would be able to see, before all else, God the Creator Himself. In observing the beauty of a flower, we would adore God and His Divine work. We, however, generally look at the beauty of nature in an entirely different way. Greed and possessiveness always taint our gaze. We desire to be satisfied by the fragrance of flowers. We greedily want to absorb their beauty into ourselves. In other words, we want to get drunk off of their beauty like off of wine, high off of their scent like off of drugs. In short, we want to possess. Such a way of gazing at the world, regardless of whether we look at a plant, landscape, or works of art, is impure. Impurity always occurs when we want to possess something or appropriate something to some extent, even if only by a gaze. Impurity of heart means that we look at people and things as if they were disconnected from the Creator and His designs. Even our relationship toward work can become impure if we separate our work from God who is hidden in every task that awaits us, in every difficulty that we must overcome, and in any success or failure related to work. When we unreservedly surrender ourselves to work, just as we surrender ourselves to those who are close to us, we do not leave any room in our professional lives for God and His plans. Moreover, our work begins to enslave us.

The relationship that saints have to the tasks at hand, and also to people and their surroundings, is entirely different than ours. St. Francis of Assisi looked not only at people, but also at animals, plants, the sun, rain and fire in a different way than we look at them. He looked at everything as God looks at the world. Purity of heart is a relationship to the world that acknowledges the place in the world that truly belongs to the Creator and Lord of everything. Purity of heart is respect for God's plan, in any given moment, for each creature. Likewise, with regard to our neighbor, purity of heart consists in respecting God, who is hidden in our neighbor and who has His own holy plan for him.

Striving for purity of heart demands that we continually work on ourselves. Maintaining purity of heart requires active renunciation. We must always strive to improve so that we have good intentions in everything that we do. However, if God's light of truth exposes a little of the mystery of the interior of the whitewashed tomb and allows you to see your spiritual misery, then you will begin to understand that you are too weak to live by the virtue of chastity on your own.

Did the prodigal son, a dirty caretaker of swine, who squandered all of his inheritance and found himself at the rock bottom of his misery, count on being pure on his own? No. He knew very well that he had wasted everything. He was clearly aware that he was only capable of impurity. Precisely because of this awareness, he returned to his father as a poor beggar.

On the path of spiritual poverty, the realization of the Gospel's call to "Be perfect, as your heavenly Father is perfect" (Mt 5:48), is based on our aspiration to achieve communion with Jesus Christ. If Christ Himself is not pure in us, then we will always have an impure relationship, full of egoism and human thinking as if God does not exist, to everything that surrounds us.

At the foundation of communion with Christ lies the contrition of a sinner who does not necessarily have to commit the same sins as the prodigal son in order to see that he is capable of committing them. Such a person has his sin constantly before his eyes. He returns to the Father so that he can trustfully throw himself into his Father's arms because he has discovered the evil hidden within him. If we want to live in purity, we have to strive for contrition with all of our strength and to aspire to communion with Jesus Christ. Then He Himself will be purity of heart in us. However, this kind of purity cannot be obtained by our own efforts; rather, this purity is achieved only by the true purity of Christ's Purest Heart.

IN ORDER TO GAIN EVERYTHING, IT IS NECESSARY TO LOSE EVERYTHING

God wants to lead you on the path that He chose for His Son – the path of denudation. If you do not choose it voluntarily, then God Himself, in fighting for your salvation, will have to strip you of all that fortifies your sense of self-greatness, builds your pride and, consequently, closes off your heart to Him. God fought for King Saul, who opposed Him, in this way. In this way, God continues to fight for every human soul that is irreplaceable in His plans.

Death is the last stage of denudation. If you humbly acknowledge your frailty and helplessness in the face of death, then you will cross the border of this world as you stretch out your hands to the Lord. You will become like the Good Thief who, in the last hour, acknowledged his own sins and admitted that he had wasted his entire life. Stripped completely, he trustfully turned to Christ as his rescue. He died united with God. Discovering that you are the worst does not mean that God will no longer wait for you; rather, perhaps, when you discover the truth about yourself, you will also discover that He waits for you in a special way.

Christ also wants you to consent to total denudation. He desires that you agree to walk on the same path He Himself walked. If you want to gain Everything, if you desire to be united with God, then you have to consent to lose everything else that is not God. You will lose only illusions and your dreams of greatness that your pride conjures up. By agreeing to lose these illusions, you will gain God Himself. **He awaits your consent to be denuded**. Denudation is a process that makes you weak and incapable of defending yourself against Love any longer. When you begin to seek help in your helplessness, you will hear the knocking of the One who, upon crossing the border into your world, desires to rescue you. God desires that you seek nothing other than Him. Because of God's desire, His knocking is present in your failures, disillusionments, and disappointments. He brings them about or allows these events to happen so that you can see that His will should be everything for you.

MARY, MOTHER OF HUMILITY

In Portugal there is a very small sanctuary called Our Lady of Miracles. The statue that is venerated in this sanctuary is one of Mary begging for God's mercy. Her eyes are humbly directed upwards. Her empty hands are stretched out before her. This image, which could be called The Begging Blessed Mother, demonstrates the essence of the spirituality of entrustment. Mary humbly stretches out her hands in a posture of humility, in the gesture of a beggar who knows that her existence completely depends on the alms that she receives. Mary, who is Queen of heaven and earth, forgets about her greatness and stands before God as a beggar who has nothing. The one who, by the will of Christ, is the mother of all people on earth, humbly stretches out her hands and begs for mercy for her children who crucified her Son. The empty hands of Mary show us her complete dependence on the One toward whom she humbly directs her upward gaze. Her eyes seem to say, "Lord, without you, I can do nothing; I cannot help my beloved children. Only You can do everything." Her hands express total powerlessness and helplessness. At the same time they are full of **the power of God's beggar** who, by trustfully calling out to God, is certain that she will receive mercy.

The words of the *Magnificat*, "For he has looked upon his handmaid's lowliness" (Lk 1:48), reveal the mystery of the extraordinary relationship that united Mary with God, even before she was definitively chosen to be the Mother of the Son of God. She, the Immaculate Conception, conceived without Original Sin, always lived in an immaculate way and, therefore, continually amazed God with her humility. Her entire life, even after the Annunciation and Christ's birth, overflowed with humility. Furthermore, Mary never sinned. She was always completely faithful to God. Therefore, her humility singularly pertained to the evil that, though it was possible for her to commit, never took place. She unceasingly begged for mercy. She always humbly turned to God and acknowledged her nothingness before Him.

In the mystery of the Salvific Sacrifice, the Sorrowful Blessed Mother accompanies her Son in a unique way. She received the title Mother of All People precisely at Golgotha. When Christ, with outstretched arms, begs for mercy for all of us who nail Him to the Cross, Mary stretches out her empty hands. Although her hands are not nailed to the Cross, they are fully united with the hands of her Son. The Blessed Mother's empty hands as well as her penetrating gaze fixed upon the dying Savior, portray the misery of a human and his helplessness in the face of evil and sin. At the same time, Mary's hands and her gaze reflect profound faith in the Salvific Sacrifice as well as the deep hope that everything will come from God. When standing at the foot of the Cross, Mary also took part in the Sacrifice of her Son. With faith, she awaited the grace of the salvation for the world that took place on the Cross.

We can also assume that, later on, when Mary prayed in the Cenacle with the apostles, she begged for the gifts of the Holy Spirit. She also awaited the miracle of Christ's Ascension by stretching out her empty hands and by completely acknowledging her own powerlessness as well as the misery of all of her children. Moreover, we can assume that the Blessed Mother unceasingly begs for the grace of mercy for us all. Mary is our Intercessor. She constantly intercedes for us in a posture of the same humility that made God Himself look upon her. Thanks to this attitude, God constantly outpours His infinite mercy on those who open themselves to Mary's love.

The Portuguese statue of Our Lady of Miracles expresses the essence of the prayer of empty hands and the prayer of trustfully begging for mercy. The miracles that take place in this sanctuary are God's response to Mary's prayer of a beggar. She, by interceding on behalf of her children, knows that, on her own, she can give them nothing. Her humility and her awaiting everything from God calls upon His presence and His action.

If Mary is united with God and full of grace, then it is only because God looked upon His handmaid's lowliness and He was delighted by her humility. The Blessed Mother is a perfect example of the attitude of spiritual poverty. The humility of Mary and her trustful awaiting everything from God is like a road sign for us who are traveling on the path to holiness or following a program of interior life. The gestures of empty hands and a gaze looking toward heaven portray the attitude of the poor and humble Handmaid of the Lord. It is recommended that everyone imitate this attitude.

Certainly the attitude of poverty is not about external forms. The tax collector who was praying in the temple stood before the Lord with head lowered because he did not dare to raise his eyes. However, surely his heart called out to God and his soul stood in God's presence with empty hands.

Miracles associated with the Portuguese sanctuary surely come not only from the intercession of Mary, Mother of Humility, but also because those who call upon her for special help attempt to imitate her attitude. Just like Mary, they extend their empty hands to God and beg for mercy after they have acknowledged their misery and helplessness. Then they are healed. After all, when Christ accomplished the miracles described in the Gospels, He repeatedly stressed that faith heals. The imitation of the begging Blessed Mother, of the Blessed Mother who performs miracles, allows us to open ourselves fully to God's mercy. By this gesture of humble begging in our intention, Mary, Mother of Humility, obtains for us the gift of humility and of self-lowering. Without this gift, as Dietrich von Hildebrand stresses, "all other virtues and good works are valueless."[45] Humility indeed, or the lowering of oneself, is ". . . the *precondition* and basic presupposition for the genuineness, the beauty, and the truth of all virtue. . . . On the degree of our humility depends the measure in which we shall achieve freedom to participate in God's life and make it possible for

---

[45] Dietrich von Hildebrand, *Transformation in Christ*, (New York: Longmans, Green, 1948; repr. Manchester, NH: Sophia Institute Press, 1990), 149. Originally published as *Die Umgestaltung in Christus*. Citations are to the Sophia edition.

the supernatural life [we] received in holy Baptism to unfold in our souls."[46] Thanks to the intercession of Mary, Mother of Humility, the greatest miracle of this world takes place: a person of *flesh, who is sold into slavery to sin,* gradually unites himself to God and, despite various forms of his enslavement, he will definitively be united with Him.

The time will come when the One who knocks will cease to be a Divine Beggar. He will no longer have to persistently knock on the door of your heart because your interior will be fully open to Him. No longer will there be two, but One. You will be unable to live without the Divine light of love. This light will embrace you and transform you in Itself. Such is the transforming union described by St. Teresa of Avila and St. John of the Cross.[47] This union takes place when the will of the soul and the will of God are one. Nothing separates them:

> . . . in the state of divine union, a person's will is so completely transformed into God's will that it excludes everything contrary to God's will, and in all and through all is motivated by the will of God.
>
> Here we have the reason for stating that two wills become one. And this one will is God's will, which also becomes the soul's. If a person were to desire an imperfection unwanted by God, this one will of God would be undone because of the desire for what God does not will. (John of the Cross, *Ascent of Mount Carmel* 1.11.2-3.)

---

[46] Ibid. 149-50.
[47] Cf. John of the Cross, *Ascent of Mount Carmel*, 2.5.3.

When embraced and governed by the will of God, your will will be united with His will. You will remain fully yourself, and yet you will be fully united with the Lord in a communion through which He becomes your life (cf. Gal 2:20). Christ, in His words to St. Margaret Mary Alacoque, expresses this extraordinary communion with God, which is the goal of our lives here on earth. Jesus said to Margaret, ". . . from now on [I want] you [to] live only the life of a Man-God. Live as if no longer living, allowing me to live in you. Because I am your life, and you will live only in me, I want you to act as if not acting: allowing me to act in you and for you, letting me take care of everything. You should live as if you did not have your own will, and by not having any, let my will be in you everywhere in all things."[48]

---

[48] Saint Marguerite-Marie, *Sa vie par elle-même*, 65, (Paris: Editions Saint Paul, 1979), 94. Editor's translation of ". . .*afin que tu ne vives plus que de vie d'un Homme-Dieu, c'est-à-dire que tu vives comme ne vivant plus, mais me laisser vivre dans toi. Car je suis ta vie, et tu ne vivras plus qu'en moi, qui veux que tu agisses comme n'agissant plus: me laisser agir et opérer en toi et pour toi, me remettant le soin de tout. Tu ne dois plus avoir de volonté que comme n'en ayant plus, en me laissant vouloir pour toi en tout et partout.*"

COMMUNION OF LIFE WITH CHRIST THROUGH MARY

IN THE ARMS OF MARY FOUNDATION
P. O. Box 271987
Fort Collins, CO 80527-1987

If this book has helped you to appreciate God's immense love and mercy, please consider donating to **In the Arms of Mary Foundation**, a 501(c)(3) organization, to help spread this spirituality (Communion of Life with Christ through Mary) throughout the USA and the world. Send donation checks or money orders payable to **In the Arms of Mary Foundation** to the address above or donate directly on the website.

For more information about the **In the Arms of Mary Foundation** or to obtain additional books, holy cards, free downloads of *Reflections on Faith* topics, or to sign up for the Quote of the Day, please visit the website at **www.IntheArmsofMary.org**.

FAITH SHARING GUIDELINES

RECOMMENDED GUIDELINES

The "Decalogue for Faith Sharing" is recommended by the Families of Nazareth Movement USA for use with this book at small group meetings. It guides the participants in a group to share their personal reflections as a response to reading the text.

RECOMMENDED PRAYER AFTER SHARING

The prayer below is recited by an individual at the conclusion of their personal sharing. This becomes a signal to others that they may now share. It allows a person to express their thoughts completely without interruption.

PRAYER AFTER SHARING

Thank you, God, for allowing me to see the truth about my weaknesses and how it calls upon the abyss of your merciful love.

Decalogue for Faith Sharing

1. **Meetings are led by the Holy Spirit through Mary.**

2. **The purpose of the meeting is:**
   - to become aware of my weaknesses and the truth of being loved by God.
   - to respond to the desire to deepen my faith.
   - to be open to others, my brothers and sisters in the group.
   - to share different experiences of my faith and how God is present in my life.

3. **When I go to the meeting, I will pray to God for others and myself.**
   - The prayer of empty hands or that of the tax collector is recommended.

4. **I will remember that I am God's child** who has the right to trust and await miracles.

5. **As a participant in our meeting I will:**
   - serve others and not count my own merits.
   - create the atmosphere of calm, focus/concentration and openness.
   - not impose on others my ways of thinking, reacting and perceiving.
   - avoid giving advice or solving others' problems.
   - speak from my personal "I" rather than use terms such as "you, we, us, people, we should, others do this."
   - avoid discussion and criticism.

6. **By keeping what is shared in the meeting confidential,** I will preserve each participant's freedom to share openly and protect their dignity as a child of God.

7. **I will not be afraid of moments of silence,** since I or somebody else may need time to reflect. Moments of silence provide us with unique opportunities for prayer and entrustment to God.

8. **I will remember to attentively listen** to what my brother or sister is saying in order to help them in the process of sharing.

9. **When I give a witness talk or share my faith, God's grace** is not only given to me but it is being multiplied and given to others.

10. **Above all, God expects from me humility and openness.** Even one person who is humble and open to God can create an appropriate climate during a given meeting that will spread to all participants. The most important and desirable goal is not the format of the meeting, but it is to be open to God's grace and presence.

Prayer After Sharing: ***Thank you, God, for allowing me to see the truth about my weaknesses and how it calls upon the abyss of your merciful love.***

BOOK COLLECTION BY S.C. BIELA

IN THE ARMS OF MARY
(A.K.A. PRAYING SELF- ABANDONMENT TO DIVINE LOVE)

This book is the fruit of S. C. Biela's many years of deep reflections and insights regarding the Christian spiritual life. In it he explains and refers to the various stages of one's interior life and offers a pathway to deepening one's prayer. For this very reason, **In the Arms of Mary** can serve as a resource for spiritual renewal both for beginners and those who are more advanced on the path toward a "transforming union with Christ."

GOD ALONE SUFFICES

In this book S. C. Biela expounds on various ways that an individual can grow in his interior life by letting go of the illusions of this world and replacing them with total reliance on God. The author guides his reader on a path toward complete surrender of self to the God of love.

BEHOLD, I STAND AT THE DOOR AND KNOCK

"Behold, I stand at the door and knock. If anyone hears my voice and opens the door, [then] I will enter his house and dine with him, and he with me" (Rev 3:20). This book leads the reader to discover the constant loving and merciful Presence of God. God never leaves His beloved children alone. He is always at the doors of our hearts knocking, awaiting our opening of ourselves to Him. Discover the different ways God knocks, why we hesitate to open the doors of our hearts, and what treasure lies ready for us when we do open the door to our Creator.

OPEN WIDE THE DOOR TO CHRIST

In this book Biela reassures the reader that there is a specific spiritual path that leads to a time when Christ will no longer have to knock persistently on the door of our hearts because our interiors will be fully open to Him. He demonstrates how the "key" of spiritual poverty will unlock the door through our imitation and the intercession of Mary, the lowly handmaid of the Lord. Then there will no longer be two, but One, otherwise known as the transforming union described by two Doctors of the Church, St. Teresa of Avila and St. John of the Cross. When transforming union happens, we will not be able to live without the Divine Light of Love. This Light will embrace us and transform us in Itself, where we will find true life.

THE TWO PILLARS

In *The Two Pillars* S.C. Biela presents and examines two of the most fundamental aspects of interior life: contrition and gratitude. He insightfully likens contrition and gratitude to two spiritual pillars in unexpected, thought- provoking ways. Additionally, Biela reminds us of the special gift and role of the Blessed Mother as God's instrument who assists the individual in growing in the authentic contrition and gratitude necessary when following the path to sanctity.

ANOTHER BOOK IN THIS SPIRITUALITY

THE GIFT OF FAITH by Father Tadeusz Dajczer

An international bestseller in the field of Christian spirituality, this book about the interior life is a call to abandon oneself to God according to the Gospel edict: "unless you turn and become like children, you will not enter the kingdom of heaven" (Mt 18:3). With simplicity and clarity, the author manages to draw the reader's attention and awaken the yearning to experience God and follow a specific path toward sanctity.

Listen. Put it into your heart,

my smallest child,

that the thing that frightened you,

the thing that afflicted you is nothing:

Do not let it disturb you...

Am I not here, I who am your mother?

Are you not under my shadow

and protection?

Am I not the source of your joy?

Are you not in the hollow

of my mantle,

in the crossing of my arms?

Do you need something more?

Words of Our Lady of Guadalupe
Mother of the Americas
to St. Juan Diego, December, A.D.1531

In the Arms of **Mary** FOUNDATION
COMMUNION OF LIFE WITH CHRIST THROUGH MARY
www.InTheArmsofMary.org
1-800-451-1321

Obtain 3 x 5 inch colored cards
at www.IntheArmsofMary.org.

www.ingramcontent.com/pod-product-compliance
Lightning Source LLC
Chambersburg PA
CBHW022018090426
42739CB00006BA/193